# Tensorflow: 100 Interview Questions

X.Y. Wang

# Contents

3 Intermediate 33

# Chapter 1

# Introduction

The field of machine learning and artificial intelligence has seen rapid advancements in recent years, with deep learning emerging as a significant subfield. TensorFlow, developed by the Google Brain team, is an open-source machine learning library that has gained widespread popularity for its flexibility, performance, and scalability. It has become a go-to tool for many researchers, engineers, and practitioners working on various machine learning tasks, ranging from simple linear regression to state-of-the-art models in natural language processing, computer vision, and reinforcement learning.

"TensorFlow: 100 Interview Questions" is a comprehensive resource designed to provide a deep understanding of TensorFlow and its applications. The book is divided into five sections, covering basic, intermediate, advanced, expert, and guru levels. Each section contains carefully curated questions and answers aimed at building a solid foundation in TensorFlow and deep learning concepts. The book is structured in such a way that readers can progressively build their knowledge, starting with the basics and gradually moving towards more advanced topics.

In the first section, we introduce the basic concepts of TensorFlow, including the fundamentals of Tensors, Computational Graphs, and the differences between TensorFlow 1.x and TensorFlow 2.x. The section also covers creating and manipulating Tensors, working with

TensorFlow Variables, and implementing simple neural networks.

The intermediate section delves deeper into the workings of Tensor-Flow, discussing various types of Tensors, the tf.data API, data augmentation, weight initialization, regularization techniques, and different optimization algorithms. Additionally, the section covers concepts like transfer learning, batch normalization, and the differences between supervised, unsupervised, and reinforcement learning.

The advanced section covers topics such as automatic differentiation, operation overloading, custom layers, loss functions, optimizers, multi-task learning, and the Transformer architecture. This section also deals with imbalanced datasets, learning rate scheduling, model pruning, eager execution, parallel and distributed training, and TensorFlow Extended (TFX).

The expert section explores more complex topics, such as dynamic computation graphs, TensorFlow Profiler, handling large-scale out-of-memory datasets, unsupervised pre-training techniques, advanced optimization techniques, custom training loops, Capsule Networks, multi-modal learning, meta-learning, and model deployment on IoT devices.

Lastly, the guru section addresses the design principles and trade-offs that influenced TensorFlow's architecture, optimizing TensorFlow performance for large-scale distributed training, advanced neural network techniques, real-time machine learning applications, model interpretability and explainability, and the impact of hardware trends on TensorFlow's future development.

"TensorFlow: 100 Interview Questions" is designed to be an invaluable resource for anyone interested in understanding and utilizing TensorFlow for their machine learning projects. Whether you are a beginner looking to get started with TensorFlow, a seasoned professional seeking to expand your knowledge, or an expert in search of advanced techniques, this book will provide the insights and guidance you need to excel in the ever-evolving world of machine learning and artificial intelligence.

# Chapter 2

# Basic

## 2.1 What is TensorFlow, and what is it used for?

TensorFlow is an open-source library for numerical computation and machine learning, developed and maintained by Google. It is used for building and training artificial neural networks and other machine learning models. TensorFlow has become one of the most popular machine learning frameworks due to its flexibility, scalability, and ease of use.

At its core, TensorFlow is designed to perform mathematical operations on arrays of numbers, also known as tensors. These operations can be simple, such as addition or multiplication, or complex, such as matrix multiplication or convolution. TensorFlow provides a variety of tools and APIs for defining, executing, and optimizing these mathematical operations.

TensorFlow is widely used for a variety of machine learning applications, including image and speech recognition, natural language processing, and predictive analytics. It is particularly well-suited for deep learning, a subfield of machine learning that involves training large neural networks with many layers.

For example, TensorFlow can be used to build a convolutional neural network (CNN) for image classification. The CNN would consist of a series of layers that perform operations such as convolution, pooling, and activation. These layers are connected in a way that allows the network to learn complex features from the input images. Once the network is trained, it can be used to classify new images with a high degree of accuracy.

Another example of TensorFlow's applications is natural language processing (NLP). TensorFlow can be used to build a recurrent neural network (RNN) or transformer model that can perform tasks such as sentiment analysis, language translation, and speech recognition.

In addition to its core functionality, TensorFlow provides a range of high-level APIs and tools that simplify the process of building and training machine learning models. These include TensorFlow Estimators, a high-level API for building models; TensorFlow Hub, a repository of pre-trained models and embeddings; and TensorFlow Serving, a system for serving trained models in production environments.

Overall, TensorFlow is a powerful tool for building and training machine learning models, and its versatility makes it well-suited for a wide range of applications.

## 2.2   Can you explain the basic components of a TensorFlow program?

A TensorFlow program consists of several components that work together to define and execute a computational graph. The basic components of a TensorFlow program are:

Tensors: These are the fundamental building blocks of TensorFlow programs. They represent arrays of values of the same data type and are used to pass data between operations in the graph. Tensors can be scalars, vectors, matrices, or higher-dimensional arrays.

For example, in an image recognition program, the input image would be represented as a tensor of pixel values, and the output would be a tensor of probabilities for each possible object.

Operations: These are the computational units that perform mathematical operations on tensors. Operations take one or more input tensors and produce one or more output tensors. TensorFlow provides a wide range of operations, from simple math operations like addition and multiplication to more complex operations like convolution and matrix multiplication.

For example, in an image recognition program, the convolution operation is used to extract features from the input image, and the softmax operation is used to convert the output logits into probabilities.

Variables: These are tensors that can be modified during the execution of the graph. Variables are typically used to represent model parameters that need to be trained during the training process. They are initialized with a default value and can be updated using operations like assign and assign_add.

For example, in a linear regression program, the weights and biases of the model would be represented as variables that are updated during the training process.

Graph: This is the core data structure of TensorFlow programs. It represents the computation to be executed as a directed acyclic graph, where nodes represent operations and edges represent tensors. The graph defines the dependencies between operations and tensors, and TensorFlow uses it to automatically parallelize and optimize the computation.

For example, in a neural network program, the graph would consist of layers of operations that transform the input tensor into an output tensor.

Sessions: These are the objects that execute the computational graph. A session encapsulates the state of the graph, including the values of variables, and provides methods for running operations and evaluating tensors.

For example, in a neural network program, a session is used to train the model by repeatedly running the forward and backward operations and updating the variables.

These are the basic components of a TensorFlow program. By combining these components in various ways, developers can build complex machine learning models that can solve a wide range of problems.

## 2.3   What are Tensors, and how do they differ from other data structures like arrays or matrices?

Tensors are a fundamental data structure in TensorFlow and other machine learning frameworks. They can be thought of as multi-dimensional arrays, similar to arrays or matrices, but with some key differences.

In mathematics, a tensor is a geometric object that maps one or more vectors or other tensors to a scalar or another tensor. In machine learning, tensors are used to represent multi-dimensional data, such as images, audio, and text, and the mathematical operations that are performed on them.

Here are some key differences between tensors and other data structures:

Tensors can have an arbitrary number of dimensions: Unlike arrays or matrices, which are limited to two or three dimensions, tensors can have an arbitrary number of dimensions. This allows them to represent complex data structures, such as images with multiple color channels, or video with a time dimension.

Tensors are immutable: In TensorFlow, tensors are immutable, meaning that their values cannot be changed once they are created. Instead, operations are performed on tensors to produce new tensors. This is different from arrays or matrices, which can be modified in place.

Tensors have a data type: Tensors have a data type, which specifies the type of data they can store. TensorFlow supports a variety of data types, including float, int, and string.

Tensors are optimized for parallel computation: Tensors are designed to be processed efficiently in parallel, which makes them well-suited for use in machine learning. TensorFlow automatically parallelizes the computation of tensors across multiple processors or GPUs, which can greatly accelerate the training of machine learning models.

Here's an example of how tensors are used in TensorFlow:

Suppose we have a dataset of images, each with dimensions of 28x28 pixels and three color channels (red, green, and blue). We can represent each image as a tensor with shape [28, 28, 3]. This tensor can be fed into a neural network, where it is transformed by a series of operations to produce an output tensor representing the predicted class of the image.

Overall, tensors are a powerful data structure that underpins much of the functionality of TensorFlow and other machine learning frameworks. They allow developers to represent complex data structures and perform efficient parallel computation on them.

## 2.4    What is a Computational Graph in TensorFlow, and why is it important?

A computational graph is a fundamental concept in TensorFlow that represents the mathematical operations that are performed on data in a machine learning model. It is a directed acyclic graph (DAG) that consists of nodes and edges, where nodes represent operations and edges represent the flow of data (in the form of tensors) between the operations.

In TensorFlow, a computational graph is defined using the TensorFlow API. The graph represents the structure of a machine learning model, including its input and output tensors, and the operations that are performed on those tensors. The graph is then compiled and optimized by TensorFlow, which automatically parallelizes the computation and optimizes memory usage.

Here are some key benefits of using a computational graph in TensorFlow:

Flexibility: By representing a machine learning model as a computational graph, developers have the flexibility to define the structure of the model in a way that is most suitable for the problem at hand.

For example, they can define complex models with multiple layers and nonlinear activation functions.

Efficiency: A computational graph allows TensorFlow to optimize the computation for efficient execution on a variety of hardware, including CPUs, GPUs, and TPUs. TensorFlow automatically parallelizes the computation across multiple processors or devices, which can greatly speed up the training process.

Debugging: By visualizing the computational graph, developers can gain insights into the behavior of their machine learning model and identify potential issues. They can also use the TensorFlow debugger to step through the computation and inspect the values of tensors and variables at each step.

Portability: Once a computational graph has been defined and optimized, it can be saved and loaded into different environments for inference or further training. This allows developers to easily deploy machine learning models to production environments or other devices.

Here's an example of how a computational graph is used in Tensor-Flow:

Suppose we want to build a simple neural network that can classify images of handwritten digits as either 0-9. We can define the neural network as a computational graph, where the input is a tensor representing an image, and the output is a tensor representing the predicted class. The graph would consist of a series of operations, such as convolution, pooling, and activation, that transform the input tensor into an output tensor. We can then use the TensorFlow API to train the neural network on a dataset of labeled images, and optimize the computational graph to run efficiently on our hardware.

Overall, a computational graph is a key concept in TensorFlow that enables developers to build and optimize machine learning models. By representing the computation as a graph, TensorFlow provides flexibility, efficiency, and debugging capabilities that make it easier to build and deploy complex machine learning systems.

## 2.5 What are the main differences between TensorFlow 1.x and TensorFlow 2.x?

TensorFlow 2.x is a major update to the TensorFlow framework that introduced many new features and improvements over TensorFlow 1.x. Here are some of the key differences between the two versions:

Eager execution: TensorFlow 2.x includes eager execution by default, which allows developers to execute operations immediately as they are called. This makes it easier to debug and test code, as well as write more intuitive and Pythonic code.

Keras integration: TensorFlow 2.x includes Keras as the official high-level API for building neural networks. This simplifies the process of building and training models and provides a more consistent interface for working with different types of layers and models.

API simplification: TensorFlow 2.x has streamlined the API, making it more intuitive and easier to use. Many of the older, more complex functions and classes have been removed or simplified, which has reduced the learning curve and made it easier to write and read code.

Performance improvements: TensorFlow 2.x includes several performance improvements, including support for mixed-precision training, which allows models to train faster on hardware that supports floating-point16 operations. It also includes better support for distributed training, making it easier to train models across multiple machines or GPUs.

Compatibility: TensorFlow 2.x is designed to be more compatible with other Python libraries and frameworks, including NumPy, pandas, and scikit-learn. This makes it easier to integrate TensorFlow into existing workflows and pipelines.

SavedModel format: TensorFlow 2.x introduced the SavedModel format, which is a more flexible and efficient way to save and load models. It includes support for serving models in production environments and allows for easier transfer learning.

TensorBoard updates: TensorBoard, the visualization tool for TensorFlow, has been updated in TensorFlow 2.x with new features and improvements. This includes support for profiling and debugging, as well as better visualization of graphs and metrics.

Overall, TensorFlow 2.x represents a major improvement over TensorFlow 1.x in terms of ease of use, performance, and compatibility. While there may be some initial learning curve for developers who are used to the older version, the new features and improvements make TensorFlow 2.x a more powerful and flexible tool for building and training machine learning models.

## 2.6 How do you create and manipulate Tensors in TensorFlow?

In TensorFlow, tensors are the fundamental building blocks of a computational graph. They are used to represent the data that flows through the graph during computation. Here's how to create and manipulate tensors in TensorFlow:

Creating Tensors: You can create tensors in TensorFlow using various methods, such as tf.constant(), tf.Variable(), and tf.placeholder(). tf.constant() creates a tensor with a fixed value that cannot be changed. For example, the following code creates a constant tensor with the value [1, 2, 3]:

```
import tensorflow as tf

tensor_const = tf.constant([1, 2, 3])
```

tf.Variable() creates a tensor with an initial value that can be changed during computation. For example, the following code creates a variable tensor with the value [1, 2, 3]:

```
tensor_var = tf.Variable([1, 2, 3])
```

tf.placeholder() creates a tensor that acts as a placeholder for data that will be fed into the graph during computation. For example, the following code creates a placeholder tensor with the shape [None, 3], where None represents a variable batch size:

```
tensor_placeholder = tf.placeholder(tf.float32, shape=[None, 3])
```

Manipulating Tensors: You can manipulate tensors in TensorFlow using various operations, such as tf.add(), tf.multiply(), and tf.reshape(). tf.add() performs element-wise addition on two tensors. For example, the following code adds two tensors element-wise:

```
tensor_a = tf.constant([1, 2, 3])
tensor_b = tf.constant([4, 5, 6])
tensor_add = tf.add(tensor_a, tensor_b)  # [5, 7, 9]
```

tf.multiply() performs element-wise multiplication on two tensors. For example, the following code multiplies two tensors element-wise:

```
tensor_c = tf.constant([2, 4, 6])
tensor_d = tf.constant([3, 5, 7])
tensor_mul = tf.multiply(tensor_c, tensor_d)  # [6, 20, 42]
```

tf.reshape() changes the shape of a tensor. For example, the following code reshapes a tensor from shape [2, 3] to shape [3, 2]:

```
tensor_e = tf.constant([[1, 2, 3], [4, 5, 6]])
tensor_reshape = tf.reshape(tensor_e, [3, 2])  # [[1, 2], [3, 4],
    [5, 6]]
```

These are just a few examples of how to create and manipulate tensors in TensorFlow. The TensorFlow API provides a wide range of operations and functions for working with tensors, making it a powerful tool for building and training machine learning models.

## 2.7   What is a TensorFlow Variable, and how is it different from a Tensor?

In TensorFlow, a variable is a special type of tensor that holds a mutable value that can be changed during computation. Unlike regular tensors, which are immutable, variables can be updated and modified as the computational graph is executed.

Here are some key differences between a TensorFlow variable and a tensor:

Initialization: A TensorFlow variable must be initialized with an initial value, which can be a tensor or a constant. For example, the following code initializes a variable with the value [1, 2, 3]:

```
import tensorflow as tf

variable = tf.Variable([1, 2, 3])
```

Updating: A TensorFlow variable can be updated using operations like assign() or assign_add(). For example, the following code updates a variable by adding 1 to its value:

```
update_op = variable.assign_add([1, 1, 1])
```

Scope: A TensorFlow variable is scoped to the graph that it is defined in, and can only be accessed within that scope. For example, the following code defines a variable within a scope:

```
import tensorflow as tf

with tf.variable_scope("my_scope"):
    variable = tf.Variable([1, 2, 3])
```

Saving and Restoring: A TensorFlow variable can be saved and restored using the Saver object. For example, the following code saves a variable to a checkpoint file:

```
saver = tf.train.Saver()
saver.save(sess, "/tmp/model.ckpt")
```

Overall, a TensorFlow variable is a useful tool for representing mutable state in a computational graph. It can be used to store model parameters that need to be updated during training, or to represent other types of mutable data that are used during computation. In contrast, a tensor represents an immutable value that is used as input or output to operations in the computational graph.

## 2.8   What is a TensorFlow Session (in TensorFlow 1.x) or a TensorFlow Function (in TensorFlow 2.x), and why are they needed?

In TensorFlow, a session is an object that represents the environment in which a computational graph is executed. In TensorFlow 1.x, sessions are used to run the computational graph and perform computations on the tensors. In TensorFlow 2.x, functions replace sessions as the way to execute a graph.

Here's how sessions and functions work in TensorFlow:

Sessions in TensorFlow 1.x: In TensorFlow 1.x, a session is created using the tf.Session() function. Once a session is created, the computational graph can be run by calling the session.run() method and passing in the tensors to be computed.

For example, the following code defines a simple graph and runs it in a session:

```
import tensorflow as tf

# Define a computational graph
a = tf.constant(2)
b = tf.constant(3)
c = tf.add(a, b)

# Create a session and run the graph
with tf.Session() as sess:
    result = sess.run(c)
    print(result)
```

Functions in TensorFlow 2.x: In TensorFlow 2.x, functions replace sessions as the way to execute a graph. A function is created using the tf.function() decorator, which compiles a TensorFlow graph into a callable Python function. The resulting function can be called like any other Python function, and it will run the graph and return the result.

For example, the following code defines a simple graph and runs it as a function in TensorFlow 2.x:

```
import tensorflow as tf

# Define a computational graph
@tf.function
def add(a, b):
    return tf.add(a, b)

# Run the graph as a function
result = add(2, 3)
print(result)
```

Sessions and functions are needed in TensorFlow because they provide the environment for executing a computational graph. They allow developers to define complex models and computations, and then execute them efficiently using TensorFlow's optimized graph ex-

ecution engine. Sessions and functions also provide a way to manage
the state of the graph, including the values of variables, which can
be updated during computation. By encapsulating the graph and its
state in a session or function, TensorFlow provides a powerful and
flexible platform for building and training machine learning models.

## 2.9    What is the purpose of using Tensor-Flow's GradientTape, and how does it work?

In TensorFlow, the GradientTape is a tool used for automatic differentiation, which is a technique used in machine learning to calculate
the gradients of a function with respect to its input variables. The
GradientTape is a powerful and flexible way to calculate gradients for
a wide range of functions, including those that are not differentiable
using traditional methods.

Here's how the GradientTape works in TensorFlow:

Recording Tensors: The GradientTape records the operations performed on tensors during computation. By default, it only records
the forward pass, but it can also record the backward pass if persis-
tent=True is set. For example, the following code defines a simple
function and uses a GradientTape to record the operations performed
on the input tensor x:

```
import tensorflow as tf

def my_func(x):
    return tf.square(x)

x = tf.constant(3.0)

with tf.GradientTape() as tape:
    y = my_func(x)
```

Computing Gradients: Once the operations have been recorded, the
GradientTape can be used to compute the gradients of the output tensor with respect to the input tensor. This is done using the tape.gra-
dient() method, which takes the output tensor and the input tensor
as arguments. For example, the following code computes the gradient
of the output tensor y with respect to the input tensor x:

```
import tensorflow as tf

def my_func(x):
    return tf.square(x)

x = tf.constant(3.0)

with tf.GradientTape() as tape:
    y = my_func(x)

dy_dx = tape.gradient(y, x)
print(dy_dx.numpy())  # 6.0
```

In this example, the GradientTape is used to compute the gradient of the function my_func() with respect to the input tensor x. The tape.gradient() method returns a tensor representing the gradient, which can be accessed using the numpy() method.

The GradientTape is a powerful tool in TensorFlow that allows developers to calculate gradients for a wide range of functions and operations. It can be used for training neural networks using backpropagation, as well as for other machine learning tasks that require gradient calculations, such as optimization and parameter tuning. The GradientTape is also flexible enough to handle complex computations and functions that are not easily differentiable using traditional methods, making it a valuable tool for machine learning researchers and practitioners.

## 2.10 How can you implement a simple Neural Network using TensorFlow?

Here's an example of how to implement a simple neural network using TensorFlow:

```
import tensorflow as tf
import numpy as np

# Define the input data and labels
X = np.array([[0, 0], [0, 1], [1, 0], [1, 1]], dtype=np.float32)
y = np.array([[0], [1], [1], [0]], dtype=np.float32)

# Define the layers of the network
input_layer = tf.keras.layers.Input(shape=(2,))
hidden_layer = tf.keras.layers.Dense(units=4, activation=tf.nn.relu)
    (input_layer)
output_layer = tf.keras.layers.Dense(units=1, activation=tf.nn.
    sigmoid)(hidden_layer)
```

```
# Define the model and compile it
model = tf.keras.models.Model(inputs=input_layer, outputs=
    output_layer)
model.compile(optimizer=tf.optimizers.Adam(), loss=tf.losses.
    binary_crossentropy, metrics=['accuracy'])

# Train the model
model.fit(X, y, epochs=1000)

# Make a prediction using the trained model
prediction = model.predict(np.array([[0, 1]]))
print(prediction)  # [[0.999]]
```

In this example, we define a simple neural network with one hidden
layer and one output layer. The input layer has two units, corresponding to the two features in the input data. The hidden layer has
four units and uses the ReLU activation function. The output layer
has one unit and uses the sigmoid activation function.

We then define the model and compile it using the Adam optimizer
and binary crossentropy loss function. We train the model for 1000
epochs using the input data and labels, and then make a prediction
using the trained model on a new input.

This is just a simple example, and neural networks can become much
more complex with many layers, activation functions, and other advanced features. However, the basic principles remain the same, and
TensorFlow provides a powerful and flexible platform for building and
training neural networks for a wide range of machine learning tasks.

## 2.11    Explain the concept of backpropa-
gation and its role in training neural
networks.

Backpropagation is a widely used algorithm in machine learning, and
specifically in training neural networks. It is a method for calculating
the gradients of the loss function with respect to the weights of the
neural network. These gradients can then be used to update the
weights in the direction that minimizes the loss function.

Here's how backpropagation works in neural networks:

Forward Pass: During the forward pass, the input data is fed into the neural network, and the activations of each layer are calculated using the current weights. The output of the final layer is then compared to the target output, and the loss function is calculated.

Backward Pass: During the backward pass, the gradients of the loss function with respect to the weights are calculated using the chain rule of differentiation. The gradients are propagated backwards through the network, from the output layer to the input layer. Each layer's gradient is calculated based on the gradient of the next layer, using the weights connecting the two layers.

Weight Update: Once the gradients have been calculated, the weights of the network are updated using an optimization algorithm such as stochastic gradient descent. The weight update is proportional to the negative of the gradient, so weights with large positive gradients are decreased, and weights with large negative gradients are increased.

Repeat: The forward pass, backward pass, and weight update steps are repeated for multiple iterations or epochs, until the loss function reaches a satisfactory level.

Backpropagation is a crucial part of training neural networks, as it allows the network to learn from its mistakes and adjust its weights to better fit the training data. Without backpropagation, neural networks would not be able to learn complex relationships between inputs and outputs, and would not be able to make accurate predictions on new data.

In summary, backpropagation is an algorithm used in training neural networks to calculate the gradients of the loss function with respect to the weights. These gradients are used to update the weights in the direction that minimizes the loss function, allowing the network to learn from its mistakes and make more accurate predictions on new data.

## 2.12   What is an activation function, and what are some common examples used in TensorFlow?

An activation function is a mathematical function applied to the output of a neuron in a neural network. The purpose of an activation function is to introduce non-linearity into the output of the neuron, which allows the neural network to learn more complex and abstract relationships between inputs and outputs.

Here are some common activation functions used in TensorFlow:

ReLU (Rectified Linear Unit): The ReLU activation function is a piecewise linear function that returns the input value if it is positive, and 0 otherwise. The ReLU function is widely used in deep learning because it is simple, efficient, and can help to prevent the vanishing gradient problem. The ReLU function can be defined in TensorFlow as follows:

```
tf.keras.layers.ReLU()
```

Sigmoid: The sigmoid activation function is a smooth, S-shaped function that returns a value between 0 and 1. The sigmoid function is often used in binary classification problems because it can be interpreted as the probability of a positive class. The sigmoid function can be defined in TensorFlow as follows: scss Copy code tf.keras.activations.sigmoid()

Tanh (Hyperbolic Tangent): The tanh activation function is a smooth, S-shaped function that returns a value between -1 and 1. The tanh function is often used in recurrent neural networks because it can help to prevent the exploding gradient problem. The tanh function can be defined in TensorFlow as follows:

```
tf.keras.activations.tanh()
```

Softmax: The softmax activation function is used in the output layer of a neural network to produce a probability distribution over multiple classes. The softmax function normalizes the outputs of the previous layer so that they sum to 1, and then applies the exponential function to each output. The softmax function can be defined in TensorFlow as follows:

```
tf.keras.activations.softmax()
```

There are many other activation functions that can be used in TensorFlow, including the Leaky ReLU, ELU, and Swish functions. The choice of activation function depends on the specific problem being solved and the architecture of the neural network.

## 2.13 What is the purpose of using loss functions in TensorFlow, and can you name a few common examples?

In TensorFlow, a loss function is a function that measures the difference between the predicted output of a neural network and the true output. The purpose of using loss functions is to provide feedback to the network during training, so that it can adjust its weights and biases to improve its predictions.

Here are some common loss functions used in TensorFlow:

Mean Squared Error (MSE): The mean squared error is a common loss function used for regression problems. It measures the average squared difference between the predicted output and the true output. The MSE can be defined in TensorFlow as follows:

```
tf.losses.mean_squared_error()
```

Binary Crossentropy: The binary crossentropy loss function is commonly used for binary classification problems. It measures the difference between the predicted probability of the positive class and the true probability of the positive class. The binary crossentropy can be defined in TensorFlow as follows:

```
tf.losses.binary_crossentropy()
```

Categorical Crossentropy: The categorical crossentropy loss function is used for multiclass classification problems. It measures the difference between the predicted probability distribution over multiple classes and the true probability distribution. The categorical crossentropy can be defined in TensorFlow as follows:

```
tf.losses.categorical_crossentropy()
```

Sparse Categorical Crossentropy: The sparse categorical crossentropy loss function is similar to the categorical crossentropy, but is used when the true labels are integers rather than one-hot encoded vectors. The sparse categorical crossentropy can be defined in TensorFlow as follows:

```
tf.losses.sparse_categorical_crossentropy()
```

There are many other loss functions that can be used in TensorFlow, including the Huber loss, KL divergence, and hinge loss. The choice of loss function depends on the specific problem being solved and the nature of the data. The goal is to choose a loss function that encourages the neural network to learn the desired patterns in the data and make accurate predictions on new data.

## 2.14   How do you choose and apply an optimizer in TensorFlow to minimize the loss function?

In TensorFlow, an optimizer is an algorithm used to update the weights and biases of a neural network during training in order to minimize the loss function. There are many different optimizers available in TensorFlow, and the choice of optimizer can have a significant impact on the performance of the neural network.

Here are the general steps for choosing and applying an optimizer in TensorFlow:

Choose an Optimizer: There are several popular optimizers available in TensorFlow, including stochastic gradient descent (SGD), Adam, Adagrad, RMSProp, and more. The choice of optimizer depends on the specific problem being solved and the characteristics of the data. Generally, Adam is a good default optimizer to start with.

Define the Optimizer: Once an optimizer has been chosen, it must be defined in TensorFlow using the appropriate function. For example, to define the Adam optimizer with a learning rate of 0.001, we can use the following code:

```
optimizer = tf.optimizers.Adam(learning_rate=0.001)
```

Compile the Model: After defining the optimizer, it must be applied to the neural network during the model compilation phase. This is done using the compile() method of the tf.keras.Model class. The optimizer is passed to the compile() method as an argument, along with the loss function and any additional metrics to be tracked during training. For example:

```
model.compile(optimizer=optimizer, loss='mse', metrics=['accuracy'])
```

Train the Model: Finally, the neural network is trained using the fit() method of the tf.keras.Model class. During training, the optimizer is used to update the weights and biases of the network in order to minimize the loss function. For example:

```
history = model.fit(x_train, y_train, epochs=100, validation_data=(
    x_val, y_val))
```

During training, the optimizer calculates the gradients of the loss function with respect to the weights and biases, and updates them in the direction that minimizes the loss. The learning rate determines the size of the update, and can have a significant impact on the performance of the optimizer.

In summary, to choose and apply an optimizer in TensorFlow, the optimizer must be chosen, defined, applied to the neural network during the model compilation phase, and used to update the weights and biases during training. The choice of optimizer depends on the specific problem being solved and the characteristics of the data, and can have a significant impact on the performance of the neural network.

## 2.15   What is overfitting, and how can you prevent it in a TensorFlow model?

Overfitting is a common problem in machine learning, where a model performs well on the training data but poorly on new, unseen data. Overfitting occurs when the model is too complex and is able to memorize the noise in the training data rather than learn the underlying patterns that generalize to new data.

Here are some techniques that can be used to prevent overfitting in a
TensorFlow model:

Use More Data: One of the simplest ways to prevent overfitting is to
use more data to train the model. More data can help to expose the
underlying patterns in the data and reduce the impact of noise.

Use Data Augmentation: Data augmentation is a technique where the
training data is artificially expanded by applying random transformations to the existing data. Data augmentation can help to expose the
model to a wider range of data and reduce overfitting.

Use Regularization: Regularization is a technique where a penalty
term is added to the loss function to discourage the model from overfitting. Two common types of regularization are L1 and L2 regularization, which add a penalty term proportional to the absolute or
squared magnitude of the weights, respectively. In TensorFlow, regularization can be added to a layer using the kernel_regularizer and
bias_regularizer arguments.

Use Dropout: Dropout is a regularization technique where a random subset of the neurons in a layer are temporarily removed during
training. This helps to prevent the neurons from co-adapting and
memorizing the training data. In TensorFlow, dropout can be added
to a layer using the tf.keras.layers.Dropout class.

Use Early Stopping: Early stopping is a technique where the training
is stopped early if the performance on a validation set stops improving. This helps to prevent the model from overfitting to the training
data by stopping training before the performance on new data begins
to degrade. In TensorFlow, early stopping can be implemented using
the tf.keras.callbacks.EarlyStopping class.

These techniques can be used in combination to prevent overfitting
and improve the generalization performance of a TensorFlow model.
The specific techniques used depend on the characteristics of the data
and the complexity of the model.

## 2.16    What is the difference between the Sequential and Functional API in TensorFlow's Keras?

In TensorFlow's Keras, there are two main ways to define a neural network architecture: the Sequential API and the Functional API.

The Sequential API is a simpler, more straightforward way to define a linear stack of layers for a neural network. It allows for the creation of a sequential model by simply adding layers one by one. For example:

```
from tensorflow.keras.models import Sequential
from tensorflow.keras.layers import Dense, Activation

model = Sequential([
    Dense(32, input_shape=(784,)),
    Activation('relu'),
    Dense(10),
    Activation('softmax')
])
```

The Functional API, on the other hand, allows for a more complex, non-linear architecture of a neural network, where the layers can be connected in any way. It is a way to define a directed acyclic graph of layers that can have multiple inputs and outputs. For example:

```
from tensorflow.keras.layers import Input, Dense, Activation
from tensorflow.keras.models import Model

inputs = Input(shape=(784,))
x = Dense(32)(inputs)
x = Activation('relu')(x)
predictions = Dense(10, activation='softmax')(x)

model = Model(inputs=inputs, outputs=predictions)
```

The Functional API allows for greater flexibility and control over the architecture of a neural network. It also enables the creation of more complex models that may have multiple inputs or outputs, shared layers, or loops. The Functional API can be used for a wider range of problems, including image segmentation, object detection, and natural language processing.

In summary, the Sequential API is a simpler, more straightforward way to define a linear stack of layers for a neural network, while the Functional API allows for greater flexibility and control over the architecture of a neural network, including the ability to define directed

acyclic graphs of layers. The choice between the two APIs depends
on the complexity of the problem being solved and the desired architecture of the neural network.

## 2.17   What is the role of a batch size in TensorFlow, and how does it affect the training process?

In TensorFlow, a batch size is the number of samples that are processed by the neural network during each training iteration. The
choice of batch size can have a significant impact on the training
process and the performance of the neural network.

The role of a batch size in TensorFlow is to balance the tradeoff
between computational efficiency and statistical efficiency. A large
batch size can make use of parallelization on GPUs and CPUs to
process the data faster, but may result in poorer generalization performance because the model may not be exposed to enough variation
in the data during training. A smaller batch size may result in slower
training times, but can provide a more accurate estimate of the true
gradient and lead to better generalization performance.

Here are some ways in which the choice of batch size can affect the
training process in TensorFlow:

Training Time: A larger batch size can lead to faster training times
because the model can process more data in parallel. However, this
may come at the cost of generalization performance.

Memory Usage: A larger batch size requires more memory to store
the data and the intermediate calculations. This can be a limiting
factor when training on GPUs with limited memory.

Optimization Performance: Different optimizers may perform better
or worse with different batch sizes. For example, stochastic gradient
descent (SGD) may benefit from smaller batch sizes, while Adam may
benefit from larger batch sizes.

Generalization Performance: A smaller batch size may lead to better generalization performance because the model is exposed to more variation in the data during training. However, this may come at the cost of slower training times.

In general, the choice of batch size depends on the specific problem being solved and the characteristics of the data. Larger batch sizes may be more appropriate for larger datasets with less variation, while smaller batch sizes may be more appropriate for smaller datasets with more variation. Experimentation with different batch sizes is often necessary to find the optimal balance between computational efficiency and statistical efficiency.

## 2.18 How do you save and load a trained model in TensorFlow?

In TensorFlow, trained models can be saved and loaded for later use. This is useful when the model needs to be used in another program or when the training process needs to be resumed at a later time.

Here are the general steps for saving and loading a trained model in TensorFlow:

Save the Model: After the model has been trained, it can be saved to a file using the save() method of the tf.keras.Model class. For example:

```
model.save('my_model.h5')
```

This will save the entire model, including the architecture, weights, and optimizer state, to a single file in the HDF5 format.

Load the Model: To load a saved model from a file, the load_model() function can be used. This function is part of the tf.keras.models module and can load models saved in the HDF5 format. For example:

```
from tensorflow.keras.models import load_model

model = load_model('my_model.h5')
```

Use the Model: Once the model has been loaded, it can be used for inference or for further training. For example:

```
y_pred = model.predict(x_test)
```

Alternatively, the weights of a trained model can be saved and loaded separately using the save_weights() and load_weights() methods of the tf.keras.Model class. This can be useful when the architecture of the model has changed and the saved weights are no longer compatible with the new architecture.

In summary, saving and loading a trained model in TensorFlow involves using the save() method to save the model to a file, the load_model() function to load the model from the file, and the predict() method to use the loaded model for inference. Alternatively, the save_weights() and load_weights() methods can be used to save and load the weights of the model separately.

## 2.19   What is TensorFlow Lite, and when should you use it?

TensorFlow Lite is a lightweight version of TensorFlow designed for mobile and embedded devices. It is optimized for deployment on resource-constrained platforms, such as smartphones, IoT devices, and microcontrollers. TensorFlow Lite provides a set of tools and APIs for converting and deploying TensorFlow models on these devices.

TensorFlow Lite has several benefits over the full version of TensorFlow. Firstly, it has a smaller footprint, which makes it more suitable for deployment on devices with limited storage and computational resources. Secondly, it can take advantage of hardware accelerators, such as GPUs and DSPs, to perform inference more efficiently. Finally, it provides a set of pre-trained models optimized for deployment on mobile and embedded devices, which can be used as a starting point for custom model development.

Here are some situations where TensorFlow Lite may be useful:

Mobile Applications: TensorFlow Lite can be used to deploy machine learning models on mobile devices for on-device inference. This can provide a better user experience by reducing latency and improving privacy.

IoT Devices: TensorFlow Lite can be used to deploy machine learning models on IoT devices for real-time inference. This can enable intelligent edge computing and reduce the need for cloud-based processing.

Microcontrollers: TensorFlow Lite can be used to deploy machine learning models on microcontrollers for ultra-low-power inference. This can enable a wide range of applications, such as gesture recognition, voice recognition, and predictive maintenance.

Rapid Prototyping: TensorFlow Lite can be used for rapid prototyping of machine learning models on mobile and embedded devices. This can help to speed up development and reduce the time to market.

In summary, TensorFlow Lite is a lightweight version of TensorFlow designed for mobile and embedded devices. It is optimized for deployment on resource-constrained platforms and provides a set of tools and APIs for converting and deploying TensorFlow models on these devices. TensorFlow Lite is useful in situations where the full version of TensorFlow is too resource-intensive, such as mobile applications, IoT devices, and microcontrollers.

## 2.20  What are some popular pre-trained models available in TensorFlow's Model Zoo, and what are their applications?

TensorFlow's Model Zoo is a repository of pre-trained machine learning models that can be used for a wide range of tasks, such as image classification, object detection, and natural language processing. Here are some popular pre-trained models available in TensorFlow's Model Zoo and their applications:

Inception-v3: Inception-v3 is a deep convolutional neural network (CNN) architecture that was trained on the ImageNet dataset for image classification. It achieved state-of-the-art performance on the dataset and is widely used as a starting point for custom image classification tasks.

MobileNet: MobileNet is a family of CNN architectures optimized for deployment on mobile devices with limited computational resources. It achieves high accuracy on image classification tasks while being lightweight and efficient.

ResNet: ResNet is a family of deep CNN architectures that use residual connections to address the problem of vanishing gradients. It achieved state-of-the-art performance on the ImageNet dataset and is widely used as a starting point for custom image classification and object detection tasks.

Faster R-CNN: Faster R-CNN is a region-based convolutional neural network for object detection. It achieved state-of-the-art performance on the COCO dataset and is widely used for object detection in a variety of applications.

BERT: BERT is a transformer-based neural network architecture that was trained on a large corpus of text for natural language processing tasks such as question answering and sentiment analysis. It achieved state-of-the-art performance on several benchmarks and is widely used in natural language processing applications.

GPT-2: GPT-2 is a transformer-based neural network architecture that was trained on a large corpus of text for natural language processing tasks such as text generation and summarization. It achieved state-of-the-art performance on several benchmarks and is widely used in natural language processing applications.

These pre-trained models can be fine-tuned on custom datasets to achieve high accuracy on specific tasks. They can save time and computational resources compared to training models from scratch and provide a starting point for developing custom models.

# Chapter 3

# Intermediate

## 3.1 Can you explain the different types of Tensors in TensorFlow, such as constant, variable, and placeholder (in TensorFlow 1.x)?

In TensorFlow, there are several types of Tensors that serve different purposes. Here are the most common types of Tensors in TensorFlow:

Constant Tensor: A constant Tensor is a type of Tensor that contains fixed values that cannot be changed during runtime. It can be created using the tf.constant() function. For example:

```
import tensorflow as tf

# create a constant Tensor with value 5
a = tf.constant(5)
```

Variable Tensor: A variable Tensor is a type of Tensor that can be modified during runtime. It can be created using the tf.Variable() function. For example:

```
import tensorflow as tf

# create a variable Tensor with initial value 5
a = tf.Variable(5)
```

```
# update the value of the variable Tensor
a.assign(6)
```

Variables are commonly used to represent the weights and biases of a neural network during training.

Placeholder Tensor (in TensorFlow 1.x): A placeholder Tensor is a type of Tensor that does not contain any values, but is a placeholder for values that will be supplied at runtime. It can be created using the tf.placeholder() function. For example:

```
import tensorflow as tf

# create a placeholder Tensor for a vector of length 2
a = tf.placeholder(tf.float32, shape=(2,))
```

Placeholders are commonly used to feed input data into a TensorFlow model during training or inference.

In TensorFlow 2.x, placeholders are replaced with the tf.data API, which provides a more flexible and efficient way to feed input data into a TensorFlow model.

In summary, constant Tensors contain fixed values that cannot be changed during runtime, variable Tensors can be modified during runtime and are commonly used to represent the weights and biases of a neural network during training, and placeholder Tensors are used to feed input data into a TensorFlow model during training or inference (in TensorFlow 1.x). The choice of Tensor type depends on the specific use case and the nature of the data being processed.

## 3.2    What is the purpose of the tf.data API, and how can you create a dataset using it?

The tf.data API is a high-level API in TensorFlow that provides a flexible and efficient way to build input pipelines for machine learning models. It enables users to easily load and preprocess large datasets, and to feed them into a model for training or inference. The tf.data API is designed to be used with large datasets that cannot fit into memory, and can handle a variety of data formats, including text, images, and audio.

Here are some of the benefits of using the tf.data API:

Performance: The tf.data API can use parallelism and prefetching to efficiently load and preprocess data, reducing the time required to feed data into a model.

Flexibility: The tf.data API provides a wide range of transformations that can be applied to datasets, such as shuffling, batching, and filtering. This enables users to customize the input pipeline to their specific needs.

Scalability: The tf.data API can handle large datasets that cannot fit into memory, by streaming data from disk or from a remote server.

Here is an example of how to create a dataset using the tf.data API:

```
import tensorflow as tf

# create a dataset from a list of numbers
dataset = tf.data.Dataset.from_tensor_slices([1, 2, 3, 4, 5])

# apply transformations to the dataset
dataset = dataset.shuffle(5)
dataset = dataset.batch(2)

# iterate over the dataset
for batch in dataset:
    print(batch)
```

In this example, we first create a dataset from a list of numbers using the from_tensor_slices() method. We then apply two transformations to the dataset, shuffling the data and batching it into groups of two. Finally, we iterate over the dataset using a for loop, printing each batch of data.

The tf.data API provides many more transformations that can be applied to datasets, such as map(), filter(), and repeat(). These can be used to preprocess data and create complex input pipelines for machine learning models.

## 3.3 How do you perform data augmentation in TensorFlow?

Data augmentation is a technique used to artificially increase the size of a dataset by generating new data from the existing data. It is commonly used in deep learning to improve the generalization and robustness of models. TensorFlow provides several tools and techniques for data augmentation.

Here are some common data augmentation techniques and how to implement them in TensorFlow:

Image Rotation: Image rotation involves rotating an image by a certain angle. This can be implemented in TensorFlow using the tf.image.rot90() function. For example:

```
import tensorflow as tf

# create an image tensor
image = tf.ones([100, 100, 3], dtype=tf.float32)

# rotate the image by 90 degrees
rotated_image = tf.image.rot90(image)
```

Image Flipping: Image flipping involves flipping an image horizontally or vertically. This can be implemented in TensorFlow using the tf.image.flip_left_right() and tf.image.flip_up_down() functions. For example:

```
import tensorflow as tf

# create an image tensor
image = tf.ones([100, 100, 3], dtype=tf.float32)

# flip the image horizontally
flipped_image = tf.image.flip_left_right(image)

# flip the image vertically
flipped_image = tf.image.flip_up_down(image)
```

Image Cropping: Image cropping involves cropping an image to a smaller size. This can be implemented in TensorFlow using the tf.image.crop_and_resize() function. For example:

```
import tensorflow as tf

# create an image tensor
image = tf.ones([100, 100, 3], dtype=tf.float32)
```

```
# crop the image to a smaller size
cropped_image = tf.image.crop_and_resize(image, boxes=[[0.2, 0.2,
    0.8, 0.8]], crop_size=[50, 50])
```

Random Image Transformations: Random image transformations involve applying random transformations to an image, such as rotations,
translations, and zooms. This can be implemented in TensorFlow using the tf.image.random_* functions. For example:

```
import tensorflow as tf

# create an image tensor
image = tf.ones([100, 100, 3], dtype=tf.float32)

# apply random transformations to the image
transformed_image = tf.image.random_brightness(image, max_delta=0.5)
transformed_image = tf.image.random_contrast(transformed_image,
    lower=0.2, upper=1.8)
```

These are just a few examples of the many data augmentation techniques available in TensorFlow. By applying data augmentation techniques, it is possible to significantly increase the size and diversity of a
dataset, leading to better performance and generalization of machine
learning models.

## 3.4 What is the concept of weight initial-ization in neural networks, and how does it affect model training?

Weight initialization is a crucial step in training neural networks. It
refers to the process of setting the initial values of the weights in
the network. The choice of weight initialization method can have a
significant impact on the convergence speed and final performance of
the model.

The main goal of weight initialization is to avoid vanishing or exploding gradients during the training process. When the weights are
initialized with very small or very large values, the gradients can become too small or too large, respectively, making it difficult for the
model to learn. This can lead to slow convergence or even model
instability.

Here are some commonly used weight initialization methods in neural networks:

Zero initialization: Zero initialization involves setting all the weights to zero. While this method is simple and easy to implement, it has a major drawback: all the neurons in the network will compute the same output, leading to symmetric weights and a loss of representational power.

Random initialization: Random initialization involves setting the weights to random values drawn from a distribution. This method is commonly used in practice and can improve the performance of the model compared to zero initialization. Commonly used distributions include uniform distribution, normal distribution, and truncated normal distribution.

Xavier initialization: Xavier initialization is a popular method that scales the random initialization of the weights based on the number of input and output neurons in the layer. This method is designed to keep the variance of the activations and gradients roughly the same across layers, leading to better convergence and performance.

He initialization: He initialization is a variation of Xavier initialization that is used with activation functions such as ReLU. It scales the random initialization of the weights based on the number of input neurons only, to account for the fact that ReLU can lead to a large number of zero-valued activations.

The choice of weight initialization method depends on the specific neural network architecture and the activation functions being used. In general, it is important to choose a method that can prevent vanishing or exploding gradients, and that can help the model converge faster and achieve better performance.

## 3.5   How can you implement various types of regularization techniques in TensorFlow, such as L1, L2, and Dropout?

Regularization is a technique used to prevent overfitting in machine learning models. It involves adding a penalty term to the loss function, which encourages the model to have simpler weights and reduces the likelihood of overfitting. TensorFlow provides several types of regularization techniques, including L1, L2, and Dropout.

L1 Regularization: L1 regularization adds a penalty term to the loss function that is proportional to the absolute value of the weights. This encourages the model to have sparse weights and can help prevent overfitting. In TensorFlow, L1 regularization can be implemented using the tf.keras.regularizers.l1() function. For example:

```
import tensorflow as tf

# create a neural network model with L1 regularization
model = tf.keras.models.Sequential([
    tf.keras.layers.Dense(64, activation='relu', kernel_regularizer=
        tf.keras.regularizers.l1(0.01)),
    tf.keras.layers.Dense(10, activation='softmax')
])
```

In this example, we create a neural network model with an L1 regularization penalty of 0.01 applied to the weights of the first layer.

L2 Regularization: L2 regularization adds a penalty term to the loss function that is proportional to the square of the weights. This encourages the model to have small weights and can also help prevent overfitting. In TensorFlow, L2 regularization can be implemented using the tf.keras.regularizers.l2() function. For example:

```
import tensorflow as tf

# create a neural network model with L2 regularization
model = tf.keras.models.Sequential([
    tf.keras.layers.Dense(64, activation='relu', kernel_regularizer=
        tf.keras.regularizers.l2(0.01)),
    tf.keras.layers.Dense(10, activation='softmax')
])
```

In this example, we create a neural network model with an L2 regularization penalty of 0.01 applied to the weights of the first layer.

Dropout Regularization: Dropout regularization is a technique that randomly drops out a certain percentage of the neurons in a layer during training. This can help prevent overfitting by forcing the model to learn more robust representations. In TensorFlow, dropout regularization can be implemented using the tf.keras.layers.Dropout() layer. For example:

```
import tensorflow as tf

# create a neural network model with dropout regularization
model = tf.keras.models.Sequential([
    tf.keras.layers.Dense(64, activation='relu'),
    tf.keras.layers.Dropout(0.5),
    tf.keras.layers.Dense(10, activation='softmax')
])
```

In this example, we create a neural network model with a dropout rate of 0.5 applied to the output of the first layer.

These are just a few examples of the regularization techniques available in TensorFlow. By applying regularization techniques, it is possible to prevent overfitting and improve the generalization and robustness of machine learning models.

## 3.6    What are the differences between Gradient Descent, Stochastic Gradient Descent, and Mini-batch Gradient Descent?

Gradient descent is a popular optimization algorithm used in machine learning to minimize the loss function of a model. There are three main variants of gradient descent: batch gradient descent, stochastic gradient descent, and mini-batch gradient descent.

Batch Gradient Descent: Batch gradient descent computes the gradients of the entire training dataset with respect to the model parameters and updates the parameters based on the average gradient. This approach guarantees convergence to the global minimum of the loss function, but can be computationally expensive, especially for large datasets.

Stochastic Gradient Descent: Stochastic gradient descent (SGD) updates the model parameters based on the gradient of a single training
example at a time. This approach is much faster than batch gradient descent, but can lead to noisy updates and slow convergence. To
mitigate this issue, the learning rate is typically reduced over time.

```
import tensorflow as tf

# create a stochastic gradient descent optimizer
optimizer = tf.keras.optimizers.SGD(learning_rate=0.01)

# compile the model with the optimizer
model.compile(optimizer=optimizer, loss='mse')

# train the model with stochastic gradient descent
model.fit(x_train, y_train, epochs=100, batch_size=1)
```

Mini-Batch Gradient Descent: Mini-batch gradient descent is a com-
promise between batch gradient descent and stochastic gradient descent. It computes the gradients of a small batch of training examples
at a time and updates the parameters based on the average gradient.
This approach is faster than batch gradient descent and less noisy
than stochastic gradient descent. The batch size is typically chosen
to be a power of 2.

```
import tensorflow as tf

# create a mini-batch gradient descent optimizer
optimizer = tf.keras.optimizers.SGD(learning_rate=0.01)

# compile the model with the optimizer
model.compile(optimizer=optimizer, loss='mse')

# train the model with mini-batch gradient descent
model.fit(x_train, y_train, epochs=100, batch_size=32)
```

In summary, batch gradient descent computes the gradients of the entire training dataset, while stochastic gradient descent and mini-batch
gradient descent compute the gradients of a single training example
and a small batch of training examples, respectively. Stochastic gradient descent and mini-batch gradient descent are faster than batch
gradient descent, but can be more noisy and require more hyperparameter tuning.

## 3.7    Can you explain how the Adam optimizer works and how it differs from other optimization algorithms?

Adam (Adaptive Moment Estimation) is a popular optimization algorithm used in machine learning to optimize the loss function of a model. It is an extension of stochastic gradient descent (SGD) that uses adaptive learning rates for each parameter.

Adam combines the advantages of two other optimization algorithms, Adagrad and RMSProp. Like Adagrad, Adam adapts the learning rate of each parameter based on the historical gradient information. Like RMSProp, Adam uses a moving average of the squared gradients to scale the learning rate.

The Adam optimizer maintains two moving averages of the gradients: the first moment, which is the mean of the gradients, and the second moment, which is the uncentered variance of the gradients. These estimates are then used to update the parameters with a learning rate that is adaptively scaled for each parameter.

The Adam optimizer has several advantages over other optimization algorithms, including:

Adaptive learning rates: Adam adapts the learning rates for each parameter based on the historical gradient information. This can help speed up convergence and reduce the amount of hyperparameter tuning required.

Momentum: Adam uses momentum to speed up convergence and reduce the impact of noisy gradients.

Robustness to sparse gradients: Adam is relatively robust to sparse gradients, which can be a problem for other optimization algorithms.

Here is an example of how to use the Adam optimizer in TensorFlow:

```
import tensorflow as tf

# create an Adam optimizer with default parameters
optimizer = tf.keras.optimizers.Adam()

# compile the model with the optimizer
model.compile(optimizer=optimizer, loss='mse')
```

```
# train the model with Adam
model.fit(x_train, y_train, epochs=100, batch_size=32)
```

In summary, the Adam optimizer is a powerful optimization algorithm that can adaptively adjust the learning rate for each parameter based on the historical gradient information. It combines the advantages of two other optimization algorithms, Adagrad and RMSProp, and has become a popular choice for optimizing deep learning models.

## 3.8    What is batch normalization, and how can you apply it in TensorFlow?

Batch normalization is a technique used in machine learning to improve the performance and stability of neural networks. It involves normalizing the inputs to each layer of the network based on the statistics of the current batch of training examples. This can help alleviate the problems of internal covariate shift and improve the generalization of the model.

In TensorFlow, batch normalization can be implemented using the tf.keras.layers.BatchNormalization() layer. Here is an example of how to use batch normalization in a neural network:

```
import tensorflow as tf

# create a neural network model with batch normalization
model = tf.keras.models.Sequential([
    tf.keras.layers.Dense(64, activation='relu'),
    tf.keras.layers.BatchNormalization(),
    tf.keras.layers.Dense(10, activation='softmax')
])

# compile the model with an optimizer and a loss function
model.compile(optimizer='adam', loss='categorical_crossentropy',
    metrics=['accuracy'])

# train the model with batch normalization
model.fit(x_train, y_train, epochs=100, batch_size=32)
```

In this example, we create a neural network model with a batch normalization layer added after the first dense layer. The BatchNormalization() layer normalizes the inputs to the dense layer based on the mean and variance of the current batch of training examples. This helps to ensure that the inputs to each layer are roughly in the same range and can help speed up convergence and reduce overfitting.

Batch normalization can also be applied to the convolutional layers in a neural network. Here is an example of how to use batch normalization with a convolutional layer:

```
import tensorflow as tf

# create a convolutional neural network model with batch
    normalization
model = tf.keras.models.Sequential([
    tf.keras.layers.Conv2D(32, kernel_size=(3, 3), activation='relu')
        ,
    tf.keras.layers.BatchNormalization(),
    tf.keras.layers.MaxPooling2D(pool_size=(2, 2)),
    tf.keras.layers.Flatten(),
    tf.keras.layers.Dense(10, activation='softmax')
])

# compile the model with an optimizer and a loss function
model.compile(optimizer='adam', loss='categorical_crossentropy',
    metrics=['accuracy'])

# train the model with batch normalization
model.fit(x_train, y_train, epochs=100, batch_size=32)
```

In this example, we create a convolutional neural network model with a BatchNormalization() layer added after the convolutional layer. This helps to ensure that the inputs to the convolutional layer are normalized and can help improve the performance of the model.

## 3.9   How can you implement transfer learning using TensorFlow?

Transfer learning is a technique used in machine learning to leverage pre-trained models to solve new tasks. It involves taking a pre-trained model that has been trained on a large dataset and fine-tuning it on a new dataset or task.

In TensorFlow, transfer learning can be implemented using the tf.keras.applications module, which provides a set of pre-trained models that can be used for transfer learning. Here is an example of how to use the VGG16 model for transfer learning on the CIFAR-10 dataset:

```
import tensorflow as tf
```

```
# load the VGG16 model pre-trained on ImageNet
base_model = tf.keras.applications.VGG16(weights='imagenet',
    include_top=False, input_shape=(32, 32, 3))

# freeze the layers in the base model
for layer in base_model.layers:
   layer.trainable = False

# create a new model by adding a global pooling layer and a dense
    layer on top of the base model
x = tf.keras.layers.GlobalAveragePooling2D()(base_model.output)
x = tf.keras.layers.Dense(128, activation='relu')(x)
output = tf.keras.layers.Dense(10, activation='softmax')(x)
model = tf.keras.models.Model(inputs=base_model.input, outputs=
    output)

# compile the model with an optimizer and a loss function
model.compile(optimizer='adam', loss='categorical_crossentropy',
    metrics=['accuracy'])

# train the model on the CIFAR-10 dataset
model.fit(x_train, y_train, epochs=100, batch_size=32)
```

In this example, we first load the VGG16 model pre-trained on the ImageNet dataset using the tf.keras.applications.VGG16() function. We
then freeze the layers in the base model to prevent their weights from
being updated during training. We create a new model by adding
a global pooling layer and a dense layer on top of the base model,
and then compile the model with an optimizer and a loss function.
Finally, we train the model on the CIFAR-10 dataset.

Transfer learning can also be combined with fine-tuning, which involves unfreezing some of the layers in the base model and training
them on the new dataset or task. Here is an example of how to
fine-tune the VGG16 model on the CIFAR-10 dataset:

```
import tensorflow as tf

# load the VGG16 model pre-trained on ImageNet
base_model = tf.keras.applications.VGG16(weights='imagenet',
    include_top=False, input_shape=(32, 32, 3))

# unfreeze the last few layers in the base model for fine-tuning
for layer in base_model.layers[:-4]:
   layer.trainable = False

# create a new model by adding a global pooling layer and a dense
    layer on top of the base model
x = tf.keras.layers.GlobalAveragePooling2D()(base_model.output)
x = tf.keras.layers.Dense(128, activation='relu')(x)
output = tf.keras.layers.Dense(10, activation='softmax')(x)
model = tf.keras.models.Model(inputs=base_model.input, outputs=
    output)

# compile the model with an optimizer and a loss function
```

```
model.compile(optimizer=tf.keras.optimizers.Adam(lr=0.0001), loss='
    categorical_crossentropy', metrics=['accuracy'])

# train the model on the CIFAR-10 dataset
model.fit(x_train, y_train, epochs=100, batch_size=32)
```

In this example, we unfreeze the last few layers in the base model
for fine-tuning, and then create a new model and compile it with an
optimizer and a loss function. Finally, we train the model on the
CIFAR-10 dataset. By fine-tuning the last few layers of

## 3.10    What are the key differences between supervised, unsupervised, and reinforcement learning, and how can you implement them using TensorFlow?

Supervised, unsupervised, and reinforcement learning are three main
types of machine learning.

Supervised learning: Supervised learning involves training a model
to predict output values from input features, given a labeled dataset.
The goal is to learn a mapping function from input variables to output
variables. The labeled dataset consists of input-output pairs, where
the input features are the independent variables, and the output values
are the dependent variables.

Supervised learning can be implemented using TensorFlow by defining
a model architecture and a loss function. Here is an example of how
to implement a simple linear regression model for supervised learning
in TensorFlow:

```
import tensorflow as tf

# create a linear regression model with one input and one output
model = tf.keras.models.Sequential([
    tf.keras.layers.Dense(1, input_shape=[1])
])

# compile the model with an optimizer and a loss function
model.compile(optimizer='sgd', loss='mse')

# train the model on a labeled dataset
```

```
x_train = [1, 2, 3, 4, 5]
y_train = [2, 4, 6, 8, 10]
model.fit(x_train, y_train, epochs=100)
```

Unsupervised learning: Unsupervised learning involves training a model
to find patterns and structure in unlabeled data. The goal is to learn
a mapping function from input variables to output variables without
using labeled data. Unsupervised learning is useful for tasks such as
clustering, dimensionality reduction, and anomaly detection.

Unsupervised learning can be implemented using TensorFlow by defining a model architecture and an unsupervised objective function. Here
is an example of how to implement a simple autoencoder model for
unsupervised learning in TensorFlow:

```
import tensorflow as tf

# create an autoencoder model with a bottleneck layer
model = tf.keras.models.Sequential([
    tf.keras.layers.Dense(64, activation='relu'),
    tf.keras.layers.Dense(32, activation='relu'),
    tf.keras.layers.Dense(64, activation='relu')
])

# compile the model with an optimizer and an unsupervised objective
    function
model.compile(optimizer='adam', loss='mse')

# train the model on an unlabeled dataset
x_train = ...
model.fit(x_train, x_train, epochs=100)
```

Reinforcement learning: Reinforcement learning involves training a
model to take actions in an environment to maximize a reward signal. The goal is to learn a policy function that maps states to actions,
in order to maximize a cumulative reward signal over time. Reinforcement learning is useful for tasks such as game playing, robotics, and
control systems.

Reinforcement learning can be implemented using TensorFlow by
defining a model architecture and a reinforcement learning objective
function. Here is an example of how to implement a simple Q-learning
algorithm for reinforcement learning in TensorFlow:

```
import tensorflow as tf

# create a Q-learning model with a neural network
model = tf.keras.models.Sequential([
    tf.keras.layers.Dense(32, activation='relu'),
    tf.keras.layers.Dense(32, activation='relu'),
    tf.keras.layers.Dense(4)
```

```
])

# compile the model with an optimizer and a reinforcement learning
    objective function
model.compile(optimizer='adam', loss='mse')

# train the model using the Q-learning algorithm
state = ...
action = ...
reward = ...
next_state = ...
done = ...
q_values = model.predict(state)
q_values_next = model.predict(next_state)
target = reward + (1 - done) * 0.99 * tf.reduce_max(q_values_next,
    axis=-1)
q_values = tf.one_hot(action, depth=4, dtype=tf.float32) * target +
    (1 - tf.one_hot(action, depth=4, dtype=tf.float32)) * q_values
```

## 3.11    Can you explain the concept of early stopping and how to use it in Tensor-Flow?

Early stopping is a regularization technique used in machine learning to prevent overfitting by stopping the training process when the model's performance on a validation dataset stops improving. It involves monitoring the validation loss during training and stopping the training process when the validation loss stops improving or starts to increase.

In TensorFlow, early stopping can be implemented using the tf.keras.callbacks.EarlyStopping callback function. Here is an example of how to use early stopping in TensorFlow:

```
import tensorflow as tf

# create a model
model = tf.keras.models.Sequential([
    tf.keras.layers.Dense(32, activation='relu', input_shape=(784,)),
    tf.keras.layers.Dense(10, activation='softmax')
])

# compile the model with an optimizer and a loss function
model.compile(optimizer='adam', loss='categorical_crossentropy',
    metrics=['accuracy'])

# create a callback for early stopping
early_stop = tf.keras.callbacks.EarlyStopping(monitor='val_loss',
    patience=3)
```

```
# train the model with early stopping
model.fit(x_train, y_train, epochs=100, batch_size=32,
    validation_data=(x_val, y_val), callbacks=[early_stop])
```

In this example, we create a model with two dense layers and compile it with an optimizer and a loss function. We also create a tf.keras.callbacks.EarlyStopping callback function and set the monitor parameter to 'val_loss' to monitor the validation loss during training. We set the patience parameter to 3, which means that the training process will be stopped if the validation loss does not improve for three consecutive epochs.

We then train the model on the training dataset and monitor its performance on the validation dataset using the validation_data parameter. We also pass the early_stop callback function to the callbacks parameter to enable early stopping. If the validation loss stops improving or starts to increase, the training process will be stopped early, preventing overfitting and improving the generalization performance of the model.

## 3.12 What are the main types of layers in a Convolutional Neural Network (CNN), and how do you implement them using TensorFlow?

Convolutional Neural Networks (CNNs) are widely used in computer vision tasks such as image classification, object detection, and segmentation. CNNs consist of several types of layers, each designed to extract different features from the input image.

Here are the main types of layers in a CNN and how to implement them using TensorFlow:

Convolutional Layer: A convolutional layer applies a set of filters to the input image, extracting spatial features from the image. Each filter slides over the image and computes the dot product between the filter and a local patch of the input. The output of the layer is a set of feature maps, where each feature map corresponds to a specific filter.

In TensorFlow, you can create a convolutional layer using the tf.keras.layers.Conv2D function. Here's an example:

```
import tensorflow as tf

model = tf.keras.models.Sequential([
    tf.keras.layers.Conv2D(32, (3,3), activation='relu', input_shape
        =(28,28,1)),
    ...
])
```

In this example, we create a convolutional layer with 32 filters of size 3x3, using the tf.keras.layers.Conv2D function. We set the activation parameter to 'relu' to introduce non-linearity in the model. The input_shape parameter specifies the shape of the input image, which is a 28x28 grayscale image with one channel.

Pooling Layer: A pooling layer reduces the spatial dimensionality of the feature maps, making the model more efficient and reducing overfitting. Max pooling is the most common type of pooling used in CNNs, which selects the maximum value from each local patch of the feature maps.

In TensorFlow, you can create a max pooling layer using the tf.keras.layers.MaxPooling2D function. Here's an example:

```
import tensorflow as tf

model = tf.keras.models.Sequential([
    tf.keras.layers.Conv2D(32, (3,3), activation='relu', input_shape
        =(28,28,1)),
    tf.keras.layers.MaxPooling2D((2,2)),
    ...
])
```

In this example, we add a max pooling layer after the convolutional layer, using the tf.keras.layers.MaxPooling2D function. We set the pool_size parameter to (2,2) to reduce the spatial dimensions of the feature maps by a factor of 2.

Dropout Layer: A dropout layer is used to prevent overfitting by randomly dropping out some of the neurons during training. This forces the model to learn more robust features and reduces the dependence on specific neurons.

In TensorFlow, you can create a dropout layer using the tf.keras.layers.Dropout function. Here's an example:

```
import tensorflow as tf

model = tf.keras.models.Sequential([
    tf.keras.layers.Conv2D(32, (3,3), activation='relu', input_shape
        =(28,28,1)),
    tf.keras.layers.MaxPooling2D((2,2)),
    tf.keras.layers.Dropout(0.25),
    ...
])
```

In this example, we add a dropout layer after the max pooling layer, using the tf.keras.layers.Dropout function. We set the rate parameter to 0.25, which means that 25% of the neurons will be randomly dropped out during training.

Flatten Layer: A flatten layer is used to convert the high-dimensional feature maps into a 1-dimensional feature vector, which can be fed into a fully connected layer for classification.

In TensorFlow, you can create a flatten layer using the tf.keras.layers.Flatten function.

## 3.13 How do you build and train a Recurrent Neural Network (RNN) using TensorFlow, and what are its applications?

Recurrent Neural Networks (RNNs) are a type of neural network that are designed to handle sequential data such as time series, speech, and text. RNNs are capable of capturing the temporal dependencies between the input data, making them useful in tasks such as language modeling, machine translation, and speech recognition.

Here's an overview of how to build and train an RNN using TensorFlow:

Data Preprocessing: The first step in building an RNN is to preprocess the data. This may involve tasks such as tokenization, normalization, and padding.

Building the Model: The next step is to build the RNN model using
TensorFlow. This involves defining the architecture of the model,
which typically consists of several recurrent layers followed by a fully
connected layer for classification.

In TensorFlow, you can build an RNN model using the tf.keras.lay-
ers.SimpleRNN, tf.keras.layers.LSTM, or tf.keras.layers.GRU layers.
Here's an example:

```
import tensorflow as tf

model = tf.keras.models.Sequential([
    tf.keras.layers.Embedding(input_dim=vocab_size, output_dim=
        embedding_dim, input_length=max_length),
    tf.keras.layers.LSTM(units=64),
    tf.keras.layers.Dense(units=num_classes, activation='softmax')
])
```

In this example, we define an RNN model with an embedding layer, an
LSTM layer, and a dense layer. We set the input_dim parameter of
the embedding layer to the size of the vocabulary, the output_dim parameter to the size of the embedding dimension, and the input_length
parameter to the maximum length of the input sequence. We set the
number of units in the LSTM layer to 64 and the activation function
of the output layer to 'softmax'.

Compiling the Model: After defining the architecture of the model,
we need to compile it by specifying the loss function, optimizer, and
evaluation metrics.

```
model.compile(loss='categorical_crossentropy', optimizer='adam',
    metrics=['accuracy'])
```

In this example, we set the loss function to 'categorical_crossentropy',
the optimizer to 'adam', and the evaluation metric to 'accuracy'.

Training the Model: Once the model is compiled, we can train it on
the training data using the fit() function.

```
history = model.fit(X_train, y_train, batch_size=batch_size, epochs=
    num_epochs, validation_data=(X_test, y_test))
```

In this example, we train the model on the training data (X_train,
y_train) for a specified number of epochs (num_epochs) and batch
size (batch_size). We also specify the validation data (X_test, y_test)
to monitor the performance of the model during training.

Evaluating the Model: After training the model, we can evaluate its performance on the test data using the evaluate() function.

```
score = model.evaluate(X_test, y_test, batch_size=batch_size)
print('Test loss:', score[0])
print('Test accuracy:', score[1])
```

In this example, we evaluate the performance of the model on the test data (X_test, y_test) and print the test loss and accuracy.

Some applications of RNNs include:

Language Modeling: RNNs can be used to build language models that predict the probability of a sequence of words.

Machine Translation: RNNs can be used to build machine translation models that translate a sequence of words from one language to another.

Speech Recognition: RNNs can be used to build speech recognition models that convert speech to text.

Sentiment Analysis: RNNs can be used to perform sentiment analysis on text data by predicting

## 3.14 What are the differences between RNNs, LSTMs, and GRUs, and when should you use each one?

Recurrent Neural Networks (RNNs), Long Short-Term Memory (LSTM) networks, and Gated Recurrent Unit (GRU) networks are all types of neural networks that are designed to handle sequential data. However, they differ in their architectures and the way they process input sequences.

Here are the main differences between RNNs, LSTMs, and GRUs:

RNNs: RNNs are the simplest type of recurrent neural network. They process input sequences one step at a time and use a hidden state to maintain a memory of previous inputs. However, RNNs suffer from the vanishing gradient problem, which can make it difficult to train them on long input sequences.

LSTMs: LSTMs are a type of recurrent neural network that were designed to address the vanishing gradient problem. LSTMs have an additional memory cell and three gates (input gate, output gate, and forget gate) that control the flow of information. The forget gate determines which information to discard from the memory cell, while the input gate and output gate control the flow of information into and out of the memory cell.

GRUs: GRUs are another type of recurrent neural network that were designed to address the vanishing gradient problem. GRUs have two gates (reset gate and update gate) that control the flow of information. The reset gate determines which information to discard from the previous hidden state, while the update gate controls the flow of information into the current hidden state.

When to use each one:

RNNs: RNNs are useful for simple sequential tasks where the input sequences are relatively short and the vanishing gradient problem is not a major concern. For example, RNNs can be used for predicting the next word in a sentence or generating new sequences of text.

LSTMs: LSTMs are useful for tasks where the input sequences are long and the vanishing gradient problem is a concern. For example, LSTMs can be used for speech recognition or language translation.

GRUs: GRUs are similar to LSTMs and can be used in many of the same applications. However, GRUs have fewer parameters than LSTMs and may be faster to train and easier to optimize.

In general, the choice of architecture depends on the specific task and the characteristics of the input sequences. It's important to experiment with different architectures and compare their performance on the task at hand.

## 3.15 What are the key elements of an autoencoder, and how can you implement one using TensorFlow?

Autoencoders are a type of neural network that are used for unsupervised learning tasks such as dimensionality reduction, data compression, and image denoising. Autoencoders consist of two main components: an encoder and a decoder.

Here are the key elements of an autoencoder:

Encoder: The encoder is a neural network that takes an input and maps it to a lower-dimensional representation, or code. The encoder typically consists of several layers of neurons that perform non-linear transformations on the input data to extract important features.

Decoder: The decoder is a neural network that takes the code generated by the encoder and maps it back to the original input space. The decoder typically consists of several layers of neurons that reconstruct the input data from the code.

Loss Function: The loss function is used to measure the difference between the original input data and the reconstructed data. The goal of the autoencoder is to minimize the loss function, which encourages the encoder and decoder to learn useful representations of the input data.

Here's an example of how to implement an autoencoder using TensorFlow:

```
import tensorflow as tf

# Define the encoder
encoder = tf.keras.models.Sequential([
    tf.keras.layers.Dense(units=64, activation='relu', input_shape
        =(784,)),
    tf.keras.layers.Dense(units=32, activation='relu')
])

# Define the decoder
decoder = tf.keras.models.Sequential([
    tf.keras.layers.Dense(units=64, activation='relu', input_shape
        =(32,)),
    tf.keras.layers.Dense(units=784, activation='sigmoid')
])

# Define the autoencoder by combining the encoder and decoder
```

```
autoencoder = tf.keras.models.Sequential([
    encoder,
    decoder
])

# Compile the autoencoder
autoencoder.compile(loss='binary_crossentropy', optimizer='adam')

# Train the autoencoder
autoencoder.fit(X_train, X_train, epochs=10, batch_size=128,
    validation_data=(X_test, X_test))

# Use the encoder to generate codes for new data
codes = encoder.predict(X_new_data)

# Use the decoder to reconstruct data from codes
reconstructed_data = decoder.predict(codes)
```

In this example, we define an autoencoder with an encoder that has two hidden layers of 64 and 32 units, respectively, and a decoder that has two hidden layers of 64 and 784 units, respectively. We compile the autoencoder using binary cross-entropy loss and the Adam optimizer, and train it on the input data (X_train, X_train) for a specified number of epochs and batch size. We then use the encoder to generate codes for new data and the decoder to reconstruct data from the codes.

Autoencoders can be used for a variety of tasks, such as image denoising, anomaly detection, and data compression. They are particularly useful when working with high-dimensional data and can learn meaningful representations of the input data without requiring explicit supervision.

## 3.16 How do you perform hyperparameter tuning using TensorFlow, and what are some common techniques?

Hyperparameter tuning is the process of finding the optimal set of hyperparameters for a machine learning model. Hyperparameters are parameters that are set before training the model and are not learned during training. They can have a significant impact on the performance of the model, and therefore, it is essential to choose them carefully.

Here are some common techniques for hyperparameter tuning using TensorFlow:

Grid Search: Grid search involves defining a grid of hyperparameter values and training the model for each combination of values. The performance of the model is evaluated using cross-validation, and the hyperparameters that result in the best performance are chosen.

Random Search: Random search involves defining a range of hyperparameter values and randomly sampling from that range. The model is trained for each set of hyperparameters, and the performance is evaluated using cross-validation. Random search is more efficient than grid search, especially when there are many hyperparameters to tune.

Bayesian Optimization: Bayesian optimization is a more advanced technique that uses probabilistic models to choose the next set of hyperparameters to evaluate. Bayesian optimization is more efficient than grid search and random search, especially when the search space is large.

Here's an example of how to perform hyperparameter tuning using TensorFlow and Keras:

```
import tensorflow as tf
from tensorflow import keras
from tensorflow.keras import layers
from sklearn.model_selection import GridSearchCV

# Define the model
def create_model(units, dropout_rate):
model = keras.Sequential([
    layers.Dense(units, activation='relu', input_shape=(784,)),
    layers.Dropout(dropout_rate),
    layers.Dense(units, activation='relu'),
    layers.Dropout(dropout_rate),
    layers.Dense(10, activation='softmax')
])
model.compile(optimizer='adam', loss='categorical_crossentropy',
    metrics=['accuracy'])
return model

# Define the hyperparameters to tune
param_grid = {
    'units': [32, 64, 128],
    'dropout_rate': [0.1, 0.2, 0.3]
}

# Create the model
model = keras.wrappers.scikit_learn.KerasClassifier(build_fn=
    create_model, epochs=10, batch_size=128)

# Perform grid search
grid_search = GridSearchCV(estimator=model, param_grid=param_grid,
```

```
        cv=3)
grid_search.fit(X_train, y_train)

# Print the best parameters and score
print('Best␣parameters:', grid_search.best_params_)
print('Best␣score:', grid_search.best_score_)
```

In this example, we define a neural network with two hidden layers of a variable number of units and dropout layers to prevent overfitting. We use the create_model function to define the model, which takes the hyperparameters as inputs. We then use the KerasClassifier wrapper to create a scikit-learn compatible version of the model, which can be used with the GridSearchCV function. We define a grid of hyperparameters to tune and use GridSearchCV to perform grid search with 3-fold cross-validation. We print the best parameters and score found by GridSearchCV.

Hyperparameter tuning is an important step in developing machine learning models. It can significantly improve the performance of the model and should be done carefully using a combination of techniques such as grid search, random search, and Bayesian optimization.

## 3.17    What is a TensorBoard, and how can you use it to visualize and debug TensorFlow models?

TensorBoard is a visualization tool that is part of the TensorFlow framework. It allows you to visualize and debug TensorFlow models by displaying various metrics, summaries, and graphs. TensorBoard can be used to monitor the training progress of your models, visualize the structure of your models, and debug issues that may arise during training.

Here are some of the features of TensorBoard:

Scalars: Scalars are numerical values that can be plotted over time. TensorBoard can plot scalars such as loss, accuracy, and other metrics to help you monitor the training progress of your model.

Histograms: Histograms are used to visualize the distribution of weights and biases in your model. TensorBoard can plot histograms for weights and biases in each layer of your model to help you understand how the model is learning.

Graphs: TensorBoard can display the computational graph of your model, which shows how the data flows through the layers of your model. This can be useful for debugging issues related to the structure of your model.

Images: TensorBoard can display images that are generated by your model during training. This can be useful for tasks such as image classification and object detection.

Here's an example of how to use TensorBoard to monitor the training progress of a TensorFlow model:

```
import tensorflow as tf
from tensorflow.keras.datasets import mnist
from tensorflow.keras.layers import Dense, Flatten
from tensorflow.keras.models import Sequential
from tensorflow.keras.callbacks import TensorBoard

# Load the MNIST dataset
(X_train, y_train), (X_test, y_test) = mnist.load_data()

# Normalize the data
X_train = X_train / 255.0
X_test = X_test / 255.0

# Define the model
model = Sequential([
    Flatten(input_shape=(28, 28)),
    Dense(128, activation='relu'),
    Dense(10, activation='softmax')
])

# Compile the model
model.compile(optimizer='adam', loss='
    sparse_categorical_crossentropy', metrics=['accuracy'])

# Define the TensorBoard callback
tensorboard_callback = TensorBoard(log_dir='./logs', histogram_freq
    =1)

# Train the model
model.fit(X_train, y_train, epochs=10, batch_size=32,
    validation_data=(X_test, y_test), callbacks=[
    tensorboard_callback])
```

In this example, we define a simple neural network for image classification using the MNIST dataset. We compile the model using the Adam optimizer and sparse categorical cross-entropy loss. We define a TensorBoard callback and pass it to the fit method of the model. The log_dir parameter specifies the directory where TensorBoard should store the log files. We set histogram_freq to 1 to display histograms for weights and biases every epoch.

After running the code, you can start TensorBoard by running the following command in the terminal:

```
tensorboard --logdir=./logs
```

This will launch a web browser with TensorBoard, where you can visualize the metrics, histograms, and graphs generated during the training of your model.

## 3.18    Can you explain the concept of model deployment and how to serve TensorFlow models using TensorFlow Serving or other deployment methods?

Model deployment refers to the process of making a trained machine learning model available for use in a production environment. Once a model has been trained and optimized, it needs to be deployed to a server or cloud environment where it can be accessed by other applications or services.

There are several ways to deploy TensorFlow models, including using TensorFlow Serving, Docker containers, serverless computing platforms like AWS Lambda or Google Cloud Functions, and custom deployment scripts.

One popular way to serve TensorFlow models is using TensorFlow Serving, a high-performance serving system for machine learning models. TensorFlow Serving allows you to deploy models to production with ease and provides several features such as model versioning, model serving over gRPC or REST APIs, and dynamic model loading and unloading.

Here are the basic steps for deploying a TensorFlow model using TensorFlow Serving:

Export your trained model as a SavedModel. A SavedModel is a serialization format that includes the model architecture, weights, and other metadata. You can export your model using the tf.saved_model.save() function in TensorFlow.

Install TensorFlow Serving. TensorFlow Serving can be installed using Docker or directly on the host machine.

Start TensorFlow Serving with the exported model. You can start TensorFlow Serving using the tensorflow_model_server command and specify the path to the exported SavedModel.

Send inference requests to the serving API. Once TensorFlow Serving is running, you can send inference requests to the model using gRPC or REST APIs.

Here's an example of how to deploy a TensorFlow model using TensorFlow Serving:

Export the trained model as a SavedModel:

```
import tensorflow as tf

model = tf.keras.models.load_model('my_model.h5')
tf.saved_model.save(model, 'saved_model')
```

Install TensorFlow Serving:

```
sudo apt-get update && sudo apt-get install tensorflow-model-server
```

Start TensorFlow Serving with the exported model:

```
tensorflow_model_server --port=8500 --rest_api_port=8501 --
    model_name=my_model --model_base_path=/path/to/saved_model/
```

Send inference requests to the serving API:

```
import requests
import json

data = {"instances": [[1.0, 2.0, 3.0, 4.0]]}
headers = {"content-type": "application/json"}
response = requests.post('http://localhost:8501/v1/models/my_model:
    predict', data=json.dumps(data), headers=headers)
print(response.json())
```

In this example, we load a trained Keras model from a file and save it as a SavedModel. We install TensorFlow Serving and start it with the exported SavedModel. We send an inference request to the serving API using the REST API endpoint and print the response.

Deploying a TensorFlow model using TensorFlow Serving provides several benefits, such as high-performance serving, model versioning, and dynamic model loading and unloading. However, other deployment methods may be more suitable depending on the specific use case and infrastructure requirements.

## 3.19  What are the main challenges in working with distributed training in TensorFlow, and how can you overcome them?

Distributed training in TensorFlow refers to the process of training machine learning models on multiple machines or devices simultaneously, which can greatly reduce training time for large datasets and complex models. However, there are several challenges in working with distributed training, such as communication overhead, data distribution, and synchronization issues. Here are some of the main challenges and solutions for working with distributed training in TensorFlow:

Communication overhead: When training a model across multiple devices or machines, communication overhead can become a bottleneck, especially when the devices are located in different geographical locations. This can result in slower training times and decreased performance.

Solution: To minimize communication overhead, you can use techniques such as data parallelism, where each device or machine works on a subset of the data and shares the model weights periodically. You can also use model parallelism, where different parts of the model are trained on different devices or machines. Additionally, you can use technologies such as NVIDIA's Collective Communications Library (NCCL) to improve inter-device communication performance.

Data distribution: When training large models, distributing the data across multiple machines or devices can be challenging. Data may need to be partitioned and distributed in a way that balances the workload and avoids hotspots.

Solution: TensorFlow provides several built-in tools for data distribution, such as the tf.distribute API. This API allows you to distribute the data and model across multiple devices or machines and provides several strategies for data parallelism and model parallelism. Additionally, you can use technologies such as Apache Hadoop or Spark for distributed data processing and storage.

Synchronization issues: When training a model across multiple devices or machines, ensuring synchronization of the model weights and updates can be challenging. Devices may have different speeds or may experience failures, which can affect the synchronization process.

Solution: To address synchronization issues, you can use techniques such as gradient aggregation, where the model weights and updates are combined across multiple devices or machines. You can also use checkpointing and recovery mechanisms to ensure that the training process can resume from a previous state in case of device failures or other issues.

Resource allocation and management: When working with distributed training, it can be challenging to manage resources such as memory, processing power, and network bandwidth across multiple devices or machines.

Solution: To manage resources, you can use tools such as Kubernetes or Docker Swarm, which allow you to allocate resources and manage containers across multiple machines. Additionally, you can use technologies such as Apache Mesos or YARN to manage resources and scheduling in distributed environments.

In summary, distributed training in TensorFlow can greatly improve training times and performance, but requires careful consideration and management of communication, data distribution, synchronization, and resource allocation. By using appropriate techniques and tools, these challenges can be overcome, allowing for efficient and effective distributed training.

# 3.20    How can you perform model quantization in TensorFlow, and what are the benefits of using quantized models?

Model quantization is a technique that can be used to reduce the memory and computational requirements of machine learning models, by representing model parameters in a more compact format. In TensorFlow, there are several techniques for model quantization, such as post-training quantization, quantization-aware training, and dynamic range quantization. Here's an overview of each technique and its benefits:

Post-training quantization: This technique involves applying quantization to a pre-trained model, without retraining the model on quantized data. This can be useful for reducing the memory and computational requirements of models that have already been trained.

Benefits: Post-training quantization can reduce the memory and computational requirements of a model by up to 4x, without sacrificing accuracy.

Example: To apply post-training quantization to a TensorFlow model, you can use the tf.lite.TFLiteConverter API. Here's an example of how to convert a TensorFlow model to a quantized TensorFlow Lite model using post-training quantization:

```
import tensorflow as tf

# Load the pre-trained TensorFlow model
model = tf.keras.models.load_model('my_model.h5')

# Convert the model to a TensorFlow Lite model with post-training
    quantization
converter = tf.lite.TFLiteConverter.from_keras_model(model)
converter.optimizations = [tf.lite.Optimize.DEFAULT]
quantized_model = converter.convert()

# Save the quantized model to disk
with open('quantized_model.tflite', 'wb') as f:
    f.write(quantized_model)
```

Quantization-aware training: This technique involves training the model on quantized data, using techniques such as weight clustering, sparsity, and quantization-aware backpropagation. This can be useful for achieving higher accuracy with quantized models.

Benefits: Quantization-aware training can achieve higher accuracy with quantized models, compared to post-training quantization.

Example: To perform quantization-aware training in TensorFlow, you can use the tfmot.quantization.keras.quantize_model API. Here's an example of how to perform quantization-aware training on a Tensor-Flow model:

```
import tensorflow as tf
import tensorflow_model_optimization as tfmot

# Load the pre-trained TensorFlow model
model = tf.keras.models.load_model('my_model.h5')

# Quantize the model using quantization-aware training
quantize_model = tfmot.quantization.keras.quantize_model(model)

# Train the quantized model on quantized data
quantized_data = ...  # Load and preprocess the quantized data
quantize_model.fit(quantized_data)

# Save the quantized model to disk
quantize_model.save('quantized_model.h5')
```

Dynamic range quantization: This technique involves quantizing the weights and activations of a model using a dynamic range that is calculated during inference. This can be useful for achieving high accuracy with minimal memory and computational requirements.

Benefits: Dynamic range quantization can achieve high accuracy with minimal memory and computational requirements, compared to other quantization techniques.

Example: To perform dynamic range quantization in TensorFlow, you can use the tf.lite.TFLiteConverter API. Here's an example of how to convert a TensorFlow model to a quantized TensorFlow Lite model using dynamic range quantization:

```
import tensorflow as tf

# Load the pre-trained TensorFlow model
model = tf.keras.models.load_model('my_model.h5')

# Convert the model to a TensorFlow Lite model with dynamic range
    quantization
converter = tf.lite.TFLiteConverter.from_keras_model(model)
converter.optimizations = [tf.lite.Optimize.DEFAULT]
converter.representative_dataset = ...  # Load and preprocess a
    representative dataset
quantized_model = converter.convert()
```

```
# Save the quantized model to disk
```

# Chapter 4

# Advanced

## 4.1 How does TensorFlow handle automatic differentiation, and how does it compare to other frameworks?

TensorFlow uses a technique called automatic differentiation to compute the gradients of a neural network with respect to its parameters during backpropagation. This allows TensorFlow to automatically update the weights of the network using an optimizer like stochastic gradient descent (SGD), without the need for manual computation of gradients.

TensorFlow's approach to automatic differentiation is based on the concept of a computation graph, which represents the computational operations of a neural network as a directed acyclic graph. Each node in the graph represents an operation, such as matrix multiplication or activation, and the edges represent the flow of data between the nodes.

During backpropagation, TensorFlow traverses the computation graph in reverse order, computing the gradients of each node with respect to its inputs using the chain rule of calculus. These gradients are then propagated backwards through the graph, allowing TensorFlow to compute the gradients of the entire network with respect to its parameters.

Compared to other frameworks, TensorFlow's approach to automatic differentiation is efficient and scalable, thanks to its ability to parallelize the computation of gradients across multiple GPUs or TPUs. Additionally, TensorFlow's computation graph abstraction allows for easy debugging and visualization of neural networks, as well as the ability to export and import models across different platforms and languages.

One notable alternative to TensorFlow's automatic differentiation approach is the technique used by PyTorch, called dynamic computation graphs. Unlike TensorFlow's static computation graphs, PyTorch's dynamic computation graphs allow for more flexible and efficient computation of gradients, as well as easier debugging and prototyping of neural networks. However, dynamic computation graphs can be less efficient for large-scale training, and may require more manual optimization to achieve high performance on GPU or TPU hardware.

## 4.2    Can you explain the concept of operation overloading in TensorFlow and give an example of how to use it?

Operation overloading is a feature in TensorFlow that allows users to define custom operations with a specific behavior when applied to tensors. This can be useful for implementing new mathematical functions or operations that are not already built into TensorFlow.

To define a custom operation in TensorFlow, you can use the tf.py_function() function, which allows you to wrap a Python function and use it as a TensorFlow operation. The function should take tensor inputs as arguments and return tensor outputs. You can also specify the input and output data types using the dtype parameter.

Here is an example of how to define a custom operation in TensorFlow using operation overloading:

```
import tensorflow as tf
```

```
@tf.function
def squared_difference(x, y):
    return tf.square(x - y)

# Define tensors
a = tf.constant([1, 2, 3])
b = tf.constant([4, 5, 6])

# Use the custom operation
c = squared_difference(a, b)

# Print the result
print(c)
```

In this example, we define a custom operation called squared_difference, which takes two tensors as inputs and returns their element-wise squared difference. We use the @tf.function decorator to tell Tensor-Flow to compile the function for better performance.

We then create two constant tensors a and b, and apply the squared_difference operation to them to get a new tensor c. Finally, we print the result, which should be [9, 9, 9].

Using operation overloading in TensorFlow can be a powerful way to extend the functionality of the framework and implement custom operations that are specific to your use case. However, it's important to keep in mind that defining custom operations can be more complex than using built-in operations, and may require more testing and optimization to achieve good performance.

## 4.3  How do you implement custom layers, loss functions, and optimizers in TensorFlow?

In TensorFlow, it's possible to define custom layers, loss functions, and optimizers using the tf.keras API or the lower-level tf.Module and tf.GradientTape APIs. Here's how to implement each one:

Custom Layers: To define a custom layer in TensorFlow, you can create a new class that inherits from tf.keras.layers.Layer, and implement the __init__() and call() methods. The __init__() method is used to initialize any trainable parameters for the layer, while the call() method is used to define the forward pass of the layer.

Here's an example of a custom layer that performs batch normalization:

```
import tensorflow as tf

class BatchNormalization(tf.keras.layers.Layer):
def __init__(self, epsilon=1e-5, momentum=0.9):
super(BatchNormalization, self).__init__()
self.epsilon = epsilon
self.momentum = momentum

def build(self, input_shape):
    self.gamma = self.add_weight(name='gamma', shape=input_shape
        [-1:], initializer=tf.ones_initializer(), trainable=True)
    self.beta = self.add_weight(name='beta', shape=input_shape[-1:],
        initializer=tf.zeros_initializer(), trainable=True)
    self.running_mean = self.add_weight(name='running_mean', shape=
        input_shape[-1:], initializer=tf.zeros_initializer(),
        trainable=False)
    self.running_var = self.add_weight(name='running_var', shape=
        input_shape[-1:], initializer=tf.ones_initializer(),
        trainable=False)

def call(self, inputs, training=False):
if training:
    batch_mean, batch_var = tf.nn.moments(inputs, axes=[0,1,2],
        keepdims=False)
    self.running_mean.assign(self.momentum * self.running_mean + (1.0
        - self.momentum) * batch_mean)
    self.running_var.assign(self.momentum * self.running_var + (1.0 -
        self.momentum) * batch_var)
else:
    batch_mean = self.running_mean
    batch_var = self.running_var

normalized = tf.nn.batch_normalization(inputs, batch_mean, batch_var
    , self.beta, self.gamma, self.epsilon)
return normalized
```

In this example, we define a custom layer called BatchNormalization, which performs batch normalization on the input tensor. We implement the ___init___() method to set the parameters epsilon and momentum, and the build() method to initialize the trainable parameters gamma and beta, as well as the non-trainable parameters running_mean and running_var. We then implement the call() method to perform the batch normalization operation, using the TensorFlow functions tf.nn.moments() and tf.nn.batch_normalization().

Custom Loss Functions: To define a custom loss function in Tensor-Flow, you can create a new function that takes the true labels and predicted labels as inputs, and returns a scalar tensor representing the loss. You can use any TensorFlow functions or operations within the function to define the loss.

Here's an example of a custom loss function that calculates the mean squared error (MSE) between the true and predicted labels:

```
import tensorflow as tf

def mean_squared_error(y_true, y_pred):
    mse = tf.reduce_mean(tf.square(y_true - y_pred))
    return mse
```

In this example, we define a custom loss function called mean_squared_error, which takes the true labels y_true and predicted labels y_pred as inputs, and computes the mean squared error between them using the TensorFlow functions tf.square() and tf.reduce_mean().

## 4.4 How can you implement multi-task learning in TensorFlow, and what are its benefits?

Multi-task learning is a type of deep learning technique that involves training a neural network to perform multiple related tasks simultaneously. This approach can be beneficial when there is a common underlying representation that can be shared between tasks, as it can lead to improved performance and faster convergence compared to training separate models for each task.

To implement multi-task learning in TensorFlow, you can use the tf.keras API to define a neural network with multiple output layers, each corresponding to a different task. You can then define a custom loss function that combines the individual task losses, and use an optimizer to minimize the overall loss.

Here's an example of how to implement multi-task learning in TensorFlow using the tf.keras API:

```
import tensorflow as tf

# Define input and output data for task 1
inputs1 = tf.keras.layers.Input(shape=(100,))
outputs1 = tf.keras.layers.Dense(units=10, activation='softmax')(
    inputs1)

# Define input and output data for task 2
```

```
inputs2 = tf.keras.layers.Input(shape=(100,))
outputs2 = tf.keras.layers.Dense(units=1, activation='sigmoid')(
    inputs2)

# Combine the output layers for both tasks into a single model
model = tf.keras.Model(inputs=[inputs1, inputs2], outputs=[outputs1,
    outputs2])

# Define a custom loss function that combines the individual task
    losses
def multi_task_loss(y_true, y_pred):
    loss1 = tf.keras.losses.categorical_crossentropy(y_true[0],
        y_pred[0])
    loss2 = tf.keras.losses.binary_crossentropy(y_true[1], y_pred[1])
    return loss1 + loss2

# Compile the model with the custom loss function and optimizer
model.compile(loss=multi_task_loss, optimizer=tf.keras.optimizers.
    Adam(lr=0.001))

# Train the model on data for both tasks
history = model.fit([input_data1, input_data2], [output_data1,
    output_data2], batch_size=32, epochs=10)
```

In this example, we define a neural network with two output layers, each corresponding to a different task. We then define a custom loss function multi_task_loss that combines the individual losses for each task, and compile the model with an optimizer. Finally, we train the model on data for both tasks.

The benefits of multi-task learning include improved performance on individual tasks, increased generalization to new tasks, and reduced risk of overfitting. By sharing information between related tasks, the model can learn to extract more useful features from the input data, leading to better overall performance.

## 4.5   What are the key principles of the Transformer architecture, and how can you implement it using TensorFlow?

The Transformer architecture is a neural network architecture that was introduced in 2017 by Vaswani et al. in their paper "Attention Is All You Need". It was designed specifically for natural language processing tasks, such as machine translation and language modeling, and has become a popular alternative to traditional recurrent neural networks (RNNs) and convolutional neural networks (CNNs).

The Transformer architecture is based on the principle of self-attention, which allows the model to selectively focus on different parts of the input sequence when making predictions. It consists of an encoder-decoder structure, with multiple layers of self-attention and feed-forward neural networks.

Here are the key principles of the Transformer architecture:

Self-attention: This is the core mechanism of the Transformer architecture, which allows the model to selectively attend to different parts of the input sequence when making predictions. Self-attention computes a weighted sum of the input vectors, where the weights are determined by a learned attention mechanism.

Multi-head attention: To enhance the model's ability to attend to different parts of the input sequence, self-attention is performed multiple times in parallel with different sets of learned parameters. This is known as multi-head attention.

Residual connections and layer normalization: To help the model learn more efficiently, residual connections are added between the layers of the encoder and decoder, allowing the input to be passed directly through to the output. Layer normalization is also used to help stabilize the training process.

Positional encoding: Since the Transformer architecture does not use recurrence, it needs a way to encode the position of each element in the input sequence. This is achieved using positional encoding, which adds a set of learned vectors to the input embeddings.

Here's an example of how to implement the Transformer architecture using TensorFlow:

```
import tensorflow as tf

# Define input sequence and mask
inputs = tf.keras.layers.Input(shape=(None,))
mask = tf.keras.layers.Input(shape=(None, None))

# Add input embeddings and positional encoding
embeddings = tf.keras.layers.Embedding(input_dim=10000, output_dim
    =512)(inputs)
pos_encoding = tf.keras.layers.Lambda(lambda x: x * tf.math.sqrt(tf.
    cast(tf.shape(x)[-1], tf.float32)))(embeddings)
pos_encoding = tf.keras.layers.Lambda(lambda x: x + tf.expand_dims(
    tf.range(tf.shape(x)[-2]), axis=-1))(pos_encoding)
```

```
# Add multi-head attention and feed-forward layers
attention = tf.keras.layers.MultiHeadAttention(num_heads=8, key_dim
    =64)(pos_encoding, pos_encoding, pos_encoding, mask=mask)
attention = tf.keras.layers.Dropout(0.1)(attention)
attention = tf.keras.layers.LayerNormalization(epsilon=1e-6)(
    embeddings + attention)

feed_forward = tf.keras.layers.Dense(units=2048, activation='relu')(
    attention)
feed_forward = tf.keras.layers.Dropout(0.1)(feed_forward)
output = tf.keras.layers.Dense(units=10000, activation='softmax')(
    feed_forward)
output = tf.keras.layers.Dropout(0.1)(output)

# Create the Transformer model
model = tf.keras.Model(inputs=[inputs, mask], outputs=output)

# Compile the model with the Adam optimizer and sparse categorical
    crossentropy loss
model.compile(optimizer=tf.keras.optimizers.Adam(learning_rate
    =0.001),
    loss=tf.keras.losses.SparseCategoricalCrossentropy(from_logits=
        True))
```

In this example, we define an input sequence and a mask to indicate
which elements of the sequence should be attended to. We then add
input embeddings and positional encoding, followed by multi-head
attention and feed-forward layers. Finally, we define the output layer
and compile the model with an optimizer and loss function.

## 4.6   How do you handle imbalanced datasets in TensorFlow, and what are some techniques to overcome class imbalance?

Imbalanced datasets occur when one or more classes in a dataset have
significantly fewer samples than the others. This can cause problems
for machine learning algorithms, which may not perform well on underrepresented classes. TensorFlow provides several techniques for
handling imbalanced datasets:

Class weighting: One common approach is to assign higher weights to
the underrepresented classes during training. This can be done using
the class_weight parameter in the fit method of a Keras model. For
example:

```
from sklearn.utils.class_weight import compute_class_weight
```

```
# Compute class weights
class_weights = compute_class_weight('balanced', np.unique(y_train),
    y_train)

# Define the model
model = tf.keras.Sequential([...])

# Compile the model with class weighting
model.compile(optimizer='adam', loss='categorical_crossentropy',
    metrics=['accuracy'], class_weight=class_weights)

# Train the model
model.fit(X_train, y_train, batch_size=32, epochs=10)
```

Here, the compute_class_weight function from scikit-learn is used to compute the class weights based on the training data. These weights are then passed to the fit method of the Keras model using the class_weight parameter.

Oversampling and undersampling: Another approach is to balance the dataset by either oversampling the minority class or undersampling the majority class. This can be done using the RandomOverSampler and RandomUnderSampler classes from the imbalanced-learn library, respectively. For example:

```
from imblearn.over_sampling import RandomOverSampler
from imblearn.under_sampling import RandomUnderSampler

# Define oversampler and undersampler
oversampler = RandomOverSampler()
undersampler = RandomUnderSampler()

# Apply oversampling or undersampling
X_train_oversampled, y_train_oversampled = oversampler.fit_resample(
    X_train, y_train)
X_train_undersampled, y_train_undersampled = undersampler.
    fit_resample(X_train, y_train)
```

Here, the RandomOverSampler and RandomUnderSampler classes are used to apply oversampling and undersampling, respectively, to the training data.

Synthetic data generation: Another approach is to generate synthetic data for the underrepresented classes using techniques such as data augmentation and generative adversarial networks (GANs). This can help to increase the diversity of the dataset and improve the performance of the model on underrepresented classes.

Overall, handling imbalanced datasets requires careful consideration of the specific problem and dataset at hand. It's important to experiment with different techniques and evaluate their effectiveness using appropriate metrics, such as precision, recall, and F1 score.

## 4.7    What is the concept of learning rate scheduling, and how can you implement it in TensorFlow?

Learning rate scheduling is a technique used to adjust the learning rate of a neural network during training in order to improve performance. The learning rate is a hyperparameter that determines how quickly the model updates its parameters in response to the calculated gradients during training. A high learning rate can cause the model to overshoot the optimal values, while a low learning rate can cause the model to converge slowly or get stuck in local minima.

There are several methods for learning rate scheduling in TensorFlow, including:

Constant learning rate: This is the simplest approach, where the learning rate is kept constant throughout training. For example:

```
optimizer = tf.keras.optimizers.Adam(lr=0.001)
```

Here, the Adam optimizer is used with a fixed learning rate of 0.001.

Step decay: This involves reducing the learning rate by a factor after a fixed number of epochs or steps. For example:

```
initial_lr = 0.001
lr_schedule = tf.keras.optimizers.schedules.ExponentialDecay(
    initial_lr,
    decay_steps=10000,
    decay_rate=0.96,
    staircase=True)

optimizer = tf.keras.optimizers.Adam(learning_rate=lr_schedule)
```

Here, the learning rate is reduced by a factor of 0.96 every 10,000 steps or epochs using an exponential decay schedule.

Piecewise constant: This involves reducing the learning rate at specific intervals during training. For example:

```
boundaries = [10, 20, 30]
values = [0.1, 0.05, 0.01, 0.005]
learning_rate_fn = tf.keras.optimizers.schedules.
    PiecewiseConstantDecay(boundaries, values)

optimizer = tf.keras.optimizers.SGD(learning_rate=learning_rate_fn)
```

Here, the learning rate is reduced at epochs 10, 20, and 30, with values of 0.1, 0.05, 0.01, and 0.005, respectively.

Cosine annealing: This involves reducing the learning rate based on a cosine annealing schedule. For example:

```
initial_lr = 0.001
lr_schedule = tf.keras.experimental.CosineDecayRestarts(
    initial_lr,
    first_decay_steps=1000,
    t_mul=2.0,
    m_mul=0.9,
    alpha=0.0)

optimizer = tf.keras.optimizers.Adam(learning_rate=lr_schedule)
```

Here, the learning rate is reduced according to a cosine annealing schedule, where the learning rate starts at 0.001 and decays every 1,000 steps.

Overall, learning rate scheduling can help to improve the performance of a neural network by finding a good balance between convergence speed and accuracy. It's important to experiment with different learning rate schedules and tune the hyperparameters to find the best approach for a given problem.

## 4.8 How do you perform model pruning in TensorFlow, and what are the benefits of using pruned models?

Model pruning is a technique used to reduce the size and complexity of a neural network by removing unnecessary parameters, with the aim of improving efficiency and reducing computational resources required for training and inference. Pruning can be performed on various levels of the model, including individual weights, filters, neurons, or entire layers.

In TensorFlow, there are several methods for performing model pruning, including:

Weight pruning: This involves removing the connections with the smallest weights in a neural network. One popular method for weight pruning is the magnitude-based pruning, where weights below a certain threshold are set to zero. For example:

```
pruning_params = {"pruning_schedule": tfmot.sparsity.keras.
    ConstantSparsity(
    target_sparsity=0.5, begin_step=2000, end_step=4000,
    frequency=100)}

model = tf.keras.Sequential([
    tf.keras.layers.Dense(256, activation=tf.nn.relu, input_shape=(
        input_shape,)),
    tf.keras.layers.Dense(256, activation=tf.nn.relu),
    tf.keras.layers.Dense(10)
])
pruned_model = tfmot.sparsity.keras.prune_low_magnitude(model, **
    pruning_params)
```

Here, the prune_low_magnitude() function from the TensorFlow Model Optimization Toolkit is used to apply weight pruning with a target sparsity of 0.5.

Filter pruning: This involves removing entire filters from convolutional layers based on their importance. One method for filter pruning is to compute the L1 norm of each filter and remove the ones with the smallest norm. For example:

```
model = tf.keras.Sequential([
    tf.keras.layers.Conv2D(32, (3, 3), activation='relu', input_shape
        =input_shape),
    tf.keras.layers.MaxPooling2D((2, 2)),
    tf.keras.layers.Conv2D(64, (3, 3), activation='relu'),
    tf.keras.layers.MaxPooling2D((2, 2)),
    tf.keras.layers.Flatten(),
    tf.keras.layers.Dense(64, activation='relu'),
    tf.keras.layers.Dense(10)
])

pruning_params = {"pruning_schedule": tfmot.sparsity.keras.
    PolynomialDecay(
        initial_sparsity=0.30,
        final_sparsity=0.80,
        begin_step=2000,
        end_step=4000,
        power=2
    )}

pruned_model = tfmot.sparsity.keras.prune_low_magnitude(model, **
    pruning_params)
```

Here, the prune_low_magnitude() function is used again, this time with the PolynomialDecay sparsity schedule to perform filter pruning.

The benefits of using pruned models include reduced memory and computation requirements, faster inference times, and potentially improved generalization performance due to reduced overfitting. However, it's important to balance pruning with accuracy and to evaluate the performance of the pruned model carefully.

## 4.9  Can you explain the benefits and limitations of using TensorFlow's eager execution mode?

TensorFlow's eager execution mode is an alternative to the traditional graph-based computation model, where computations are defined in a static graph and then executed later in a session. Eager execution allows for more intuitive, imperative-style coding, where computation is performed immediately as operations are executed.

Some benefits of using TensorFlow's eager execution mode include:

Improved debugging: With eager execution, it's easier to inspect the results of intermediate computations and identify errors, since you can print and manipulate values directly during execution.

Dynamic control flow: Eager execution allows for more flexible control flow constructs, such as loops and conditionals, to be used within a computation graph.

Better integration with Python: Eager execution enables the use of Python constructs such as lists, dictionaries, and objects, making it easier to use TensorFlow within a larger Python codebase.

Easier model building: With eager execution, it's simpler to build and test models incrementally, since computations are executed immediately.

However, there are also some limitations to using eager execution:

Reduced performance: Eager execution mode can be slower than the traditional graph-based approach, particularly for large models or when running on a GPU.

Memory usage: Because eager execution stores intermediate results during computation, it may use more memory than the graph-based approach.

Exporting models: While it's possible to export models built using eager execution to the graph-based format, the resulting graphs may be less optimized than those built using the graph-based approach.

Here's an example of using eager execution mode to create a simple neural network:

```
import tensorflow as tf

# Enable eager execution
tf.enable_eager_execution()

# Define the model
model = tf.keras.Sequential([
    tf.keras.layers.Dense(32, activation='relu', input_shape=(784,)),
    tf.keras.layers.Dropout(0.2),
    tf.keras.layers.Dense(10, activation='softmax')
])

# Define the loss function and optimizer
loss_fn = tf.keras.losses.SparseCategoricalCrossentropy()
optimizer = tf.keras.optimizers.Adam()

# Train the model
(x_train, y_train), (x_test, y_test) = tf.keras.datasets.mnist.
    load_data()
x_train, x_test = x_train / 255.0, x_test / 255.0

for epoch in range(10):
# Iterate over batches
for x_batch, y_batch in tf.data.Dataset.from_tensor_slices((x_train,
    y_train)).batch(32):
  # Compute gradients
  with tf.GradientTape() as tape:
     logits = model(x_batch, training=True)
     loss_value = loss_fn(y_batch, logits)
     grads = tape.gradient(loss_value, model.trainable_variables)

  # Update weights
  optimizer.apply_gradients(zip(grads, model.trainable_variables))

  # Evaluate performance
  test_loss, test_acc = tf.metrics.Mean(), tf.metrics.
      SparseCategoricalAccuracy()
  for x_batch, y_batch in tf.data.Dataset.from_tensor_slices((
      x_test, y_test)).batch(32):
     logits = model(x_batch, training=False)
     test_loss(loss_fn(y_batch, logits))
     test_acc(y_batch, logits)
```

```
print('Epoch␣{}:␣Loss:␣{:.3f},␣Accuracy:␣{:.3%}'.format(epoch
    +1, test_loss.result(), test_acc.result()))
```

Here, we've enabled eager execution using tf.enable_eager_execution(), and then defined and trained a simple neural network using the eager execution mode.

## 4.10   How can you implement parallel and distributed training using TensorFlow's APIs, such as tf.distribute?

TensorFlow's distributed computing APIs, such as tf.distribute, allow for the efficient training of deep learning models across multiple devices and machines. Parallel and distributed training can improve model training times by distributing the workload across multiple GPUs or CPUs.

To implement parallel and distributed training using tf.distribute, we need to follow the following steps:

Define the model: We define the model architecture using Tensor-Flow's Keras API as usual.

Define the distribution strategy: We need to create a distribution strategy object that specifies how to distribute the model across multiple devices or machines. There are different types of strategies, such as MirroredStrategy, which replicates the model across multiple GPUs on a single machine, or MultiWorkerMirroredStrategy, which distributes the model across multiple machines.

Configure the input pipeline: We need to configure the input pipeline to load the data in parallel. We can use TensorFlow's tf.data API to create a data pipeline and distribute it across multiple devices or machines.

Define the training loop: We define the training loop as usual, but we need to wrap it in a tf.function to compile it into a TensorFlow graph. We can then use the strategy.run method to execute the training loop across multiple devices or machines.

Here's an example of how to implement parallel training using tf.distribute.MirroredStrategy:

```
import tensorflow as tf

# Define the model architecture
model = tf.keras.Sequential([
    tf.keras.layers.Dense(64, activation='relu', input_shape=(784,)),
    tf.keras.layers.Dense(10, activation='softmax')
])

# Define the distribution strategy
strategy = tf.distribute.MirroredStrategy()

# Configure the input pipeline
(train_images, train_labels), _ = tf.keras.datasets.mnist.load_data
    ()
train_dataset = tf.data.Dataset.from_tensor_slices((train_images,
    train_labels))
train_dataset = train_dataset.shuffle(buffer_size=1024).batch(64)

# Define the training loop
@tf.function
def train_step(images, labels):
    with tf.GradientTape() as tape:
        predictions = model(images)
        loss = tf.keras.losses.sparse_categorical_crossentropy(labels,
            predictions)
        gradients = tape.gradient(loss, model.trainable_variables)
        optimizer.apply_gradients(zip(gradients, model.
            trainable_variables))
        train_loss(loss)
        train_accuracy(labels, predictions)

# Create a distributed dataset
train_dist_dataset = strategy.experimental_distribute_dataset(
    train_dataset)

# Define the training loop across devices
with strategy.scope():
    optimizer = tf.keras.optimizers.Adam()
    train_loss = tf.keras.metrics.Mean(name='train_loss')
    train_accuracy = tf.keras.metrics.SparseCategoricalAccuracy(name=
        'train_accuracy')

# Iterate over the distributed dataset
for epoch in range(10):
    total_loss = 0.0
    num_batches = 0
    for x in train_dist_dataset:
        strategy.run(train_step, args=(x[0], x[1]))
        num_batches += 1
        print('Epoch {} Loss {:.4f} Accuracy {:.4f}'.format(epoch+1,
            train_loss.result(), train_accuracy.result()))
    train_loss.reset_states()
    train_accuracy.reset_states()
```

In this example, we define a simple fully-connected neural network to classify images from the MNIST dataset. We use tf.distribute.MirroredStrategy to replicate the model across multiple GPUs on a single machine. We then load the data using TensorFlow's tf.data API and create a distributed dataset. Finally, we define the training loop and execute it across multiple GPUs using the strategy.run method.

## 4.11 What are the main differences between TensorFlow Estimators and Keras models, and when should you use each one?

TensorFlow Estimators and Keras models are both high-level APIs provided by TensorFlow for building machine learning models. While both can be used to build a variety of models, there are some differences in their design and use cases.

TensorFlow Estimators are designed to provide a simple, scalable way to build machine learning models for production. They offer built-in support for distributed training, model exporting and serving, and other features that make them suitable for deployment in large-scale environments. Estimators also provide a higher level of abstraction compared to Keras, allowing developers to focus more on the overall architecture of their models and less on the low-level implementation details.

Keras, on the other hand, is a more user-friendly API that is designed to make it easier for developers to quickly build and prototype machine learning models. It provides a simple and intuitive interface for building neural networks, as well as a rich set of pre-built layers and utilities for common tasks such as image classification, natural language processing, and time-series analysis. Keras also has support for distributed training, but it is not as comprehensive as Estimators.

Here are some of the main differences between TensorFlow Estimators and Keras models:

Design Philosophy: TensorFlow Estimators are designed to provide a simple, scalable way to build machine learning models for production, while Keras is designed to make it easier for developers to quickly build and prototype machine learning models.

API Complexity: TensorFlow Estimators provide a higher level of abstraction compared to Keras, allowing developers to focus more on the overall architecture of their models and less on the low-level implementation details. Keras, on the other hand, provides a simple and intuitive interface for building neural networks.

Distributed Training: TensorFlow Estimators offer built-in support for distributed training, while Keras has support for distributed training but it is not as comprehensive as Estimators.

Model Deployment: TensorFlow Estimators offer built-in support for exporting and serving models for deployment, while Keras has some support for exporting models but it is not as comprehensive as Estimators.

In summary, TensorFlow Estimators are best suited for building production-ready models that require scalability and distributed training, while Keras is more suitable for quick prototyping and building models for research purposes.

## 4.12 What are the key components of TensorFlow Extended (TFX), and how can they be used in a production ML pipeline?

TensorFlow Extended (TFX) is an end-to-end platform for building and deploying production machine learning (ML) pipelines. It provides a set of components and libraries that enable teams to create scalable and maintainable ML pipelines that include data validation, preprocessing, model training, evaluation, and serving.

The key components of TFX are:

Data validation: TFX provides the TensorFlow Data Validation (TFDV) library, which allows you to define a schema for your data and validate it before training your models. TFDV can help you detect anomalies and errors in your data, such as missing values, incorrect data types, or unexpected distributions.

Preprocessing: TFX includes the TensorFlow Transform (TFT) library, which allows you to perform data preprocessing at scale. TFT provides a set of reusable functions for common preprocessing tasks, such as scaling, normalization, and feature engineering. It also allows you to apply the same preprocessing steps to both training and serving data.

Training: TFX supports both TensorFlow Estimators and Keras models for training your ML models. It provides a set of standard hyperparameters and training configurations that can be easily customized for your specific use case. TFX also includes the TensorFlow Model Analysis (TFMA) library, which provides tools for evaluating and visualizing the performance of your models.

Evaluation: TFX provides several ways to evaluate your models, including TFMA, which allows you to compare the performance of multiple models using metrics such as accuracy, precision, and recall. TFX also includes the TensorFlow Serving component, which allows you to serve your models for online inference.

Serving: TFX supports TensorFlow Serving, which is a high-performance serving system for machine learning models. TensorFlow Serving allows you to deploy your trained models to production and serve them at scale with low latency and high throughput. TFX also supports other serving options, such as TensorFlow Lite for mobile devices and TensorFlow.js for web applications.

TFX provides a standardized approach to building ML pipelines that can be easily scaled and maintained. It allows teams to collaborate on building and deploying ML models, while also ensuring that best practices are followed for data preprocessing, model training, evaluation, and serving.

## 4.13   Can you explain how to perform federated learning using TensorFlow, and what are its advantages?

Federated learning is a type of machine learning that allows for training models on decentralized data sources, such as mobile devices or edge servers, without the need to transmit the data to a central location. Instead, the data is kept locally on each device or server, and only the model updates are transmitted back and forth. This approach helps to address privacy concerns and data localization requirements, while also improving the overall scalability and efficiency of the training process.

TensorFlow provides a set of APIs and tools for implementing federated learning workflows, which can be used in a variety of scenarios, such as personalized recommendation systems, predictive maintenance, and natural language processing, among others.

The main components of a federated learning system using TensorFlow include:

Federated Data: This is the decentralized data that is distributed across multiple devices or servers, and which is used for training the models. Each data source is associated with a unique identifier, such as a user ID or device ID, which allows the data to be aggregated and analyzed across the network.

Federated Model: This is the machine learning model that is trained on the federated data, using techniques such as stochastic gradient descent or federated averaging. The model is divided into two components: a global model, which is shared across all devices or servers, and a local model, which is trained on each device or server using the local data.

Federated Learning Algorithm: This is the algorithm that governs the training process, including how the model updates are aggregated and communicated across the network. TensorFlow provides a set of pre-built federated learning algorithms, such as Federated Averaging, Federated SGD, and Federated Proximal Gradient Descent, which can be customized and extended as needed.

Federated Optimization: This is the process of optimizing the federated learning algorithm to improve its efficiency and accuracy. This includes techniques such as adaptive learning rates, compression, and quantization, which are designed to reduce the amount of communication and computation required during training.

Federated Evaluation: This is the process of evaluating the performance of the federated model, using metrics such as accuracy, precision, and recall. The evaluation is typically performed on a held-out set of data, which is not used during training, and which helps to ensure that the model is not overfitting to the local data.

Overall, federated learning offers a promising approach for training machine learning models on decentralized data sources, while also addressing privacy concerns and data localization requirements. TensorFlow provides a powerful set of tools and APIs for implementing federated learning workflows, which can be customized and extended as needed for specific use cases.

## 4.14    How can you use TensorFlow with other frameworks, such as PyTorch or ONNX?

TensorFlow is a popular open-source framework for building machine learning models, but it is not the only framework available. There may be situations where you need to use other frameworks, such as PyTorch or ONNX, for specific tasks or to integrate with existing code. TensorFlow provides several ways to use it with other frameworks, including:

Using TensorFlow with PyTorch: TensorFlow provides a library called TensorFlow-on-PyTorch (TF-ON-PY) that allows you to run PyTorch models in TensorFlow. This can be useful if you have existing PyTorch models and want to use them in a TensorFlow pipeline. TF-ON-PY provides an interface to PyTorch models that can be run in TensorFlow, with support for data loading, model conversion, and training.

Using TensorFlow with ONNX: ONNX (Open Neural Network Exchange) is an open standard for representing machine learning models. TensorFlow provides support for exporting models in the ONNX format, which allows you to use TensorFlow models in other frameworks that support ONNX, such as PyTorch, MXNet, and Caffe2. You can export a TensorFlow model to ONNX format using the tf.saved_model API.

Here is an example of how to export a TensorFlow model to ONNX format:

```
import tensorflow as tf
import onnx
from onnx_tf.backend import prepare

# Build and train a TensorFlow model
model = tf.keras.Sequential([
    tf.keras.layers.Dense(64, activation='relu'),
    tf.keras.layers.Dense(10, activation='softmax')
])
model.compile(optimizer='adam', loss='categorical_crossentropy',
    metrics=['accuracy'])
model.fit(x_train, y_train, epochs=10)

# Export the model to ONNX format
tf.saved_model.save(model, 'my_model')
onnx_model = onnx.load('my_model')
onnx.checker.check_model(onnx_model)

# Convert the ONNX model to TensorFlow format
tf_rep = prepare(onnx_model)
tf_model = tf_rep.export_graph()
```

This example builds and trains a simple TensorFlow model, exports it to ONNX format using the tf.saved_model.save API, and then loads the ONNX model and converts it to TensorFlow format using the onnx_tf.backend.prepare API.

Overall, TensorFlow provides a variety of tools and APIs for working with other frameworks, allowing you to take advantage of the strengths of each framework for your specific needs.

## 4.15  What are some common techniques for debugging and profiling Tensor-Flow models, and how can they be used to optimize performance?

Debugging and profiling TensorFlow models are essential steps in optimizing the performance of deep learning models. Here are some common techniques for debugging and profiling TensorFlow models:

TensorFlow Debugger (tfdbg): TensorFlow Debugger (tfdbg) is a built-in debugger in TensorFlow that allows developers to track the flow of tensors and the execution of operations during the training process. This tool enables users to pause the training process, inspect the values of tensors, and modify the values of tensors on the fly. Developers can use tfdbg to detect issues like vanishing gradients, exploding gradients, and overfitting.

TensorBoard: TensorBoard is a web-based visualization tool in TensorFlow that can be used to visualize the training process of deep learning models. TensorBoard provides many visualization features, including scalar summaries, histogram summaries, and image summaries. These summaries can be used to track metrics like accuracy and loss, visualize the distribution of weights and biases, and display the images processed by the model.

Profiling tools: TensorFlow provides many profiling tools to optimize the performance of deep learning models. Some of these profiling tools include:

TensorFlow Profiler: TensorFlow Profiler is a tool in TensorFlow that provides a graphical interface for analyzing the performance of deep learning models. TensorFlow Profiler can be used to identify performance bottlenecks, analyze the behavior of the GPU, and optimize the execution of operations.

CUDA Profiling Tools Interface (CUPTI): CUPTI is a set of profiling tools provided by NVIDIA that can be used to analyze the performance of GPU-accelerated deep learning models. CUPTI can be used to monitor the execution of CUDA kernels, analyze the memory usage of the GPU, and identify performance bottlenecks.

Python profiling tools: Python provides many profiling tools, such as cProfile and Pyflame, that can be used to analyze the performance of Python code. These tools can be used to identify performance bottlenecks in the Python code used in the training process.

Unit testing: Unit testing is a common technique used to ensure the correctness of deep learning models. Unit testing involves creating small test cases for individual functions and components of the model. Unit testing can be used to identify issues like incorrect tensor shapes, incorrect calculations, and NaN values.

Code reviews: Code reviews are an essential step in the development process of deep learning models. Code reviews involve having one or more developers review the code written by another developer. Code reviews can be used to identify issues like inefficient code, poorly structured code, and incorrect usage of TensorFlow APIs.

In summary, debugging and profiling TensorFlow models are critical steps in optimizing the performance of deep learning models. Tensor-Flow provides many built-in tools for debugging and profiling, and developers can also use external tools and techniques like unit testing and code reviews to ensure the correctness and performance of their models.

## 4.16    How can you utilize TensorFlow's performance optimizations, such as mixed precision training and XLA?

TensorFlow provides several performance optimizations to speed up the training and inference of machine learning models. Two of the most commonly used optimizations are mixed precision training and XLA (Accelerated Linear Algebra) optimization.

Mixed precision training is a technique that uses both lower-precision (e.g., float16) and higher-precision (e.g., float32) data types to perform the computations in a neural network. The idea behind mixed precision training is that many computations can be performed using lower-precision data types without significantly affecting the model's accuracy. By using lower-precision data types, the computation time can be significantly reduced, leading to faster training times.

In TensorFlow, mixed precision training can be implemented using the tf.keras.mixed_precision API. This API allows you to define a policy for each variable in the model, indicating whether it should be stored and used in lower-precision or higher-precision data types. Here's an example:

```
import tensorflow as tf

# Enable mixed precision training
tf.keras.mixed_precision.set_global_policy('mixed_float16')

# Build and train a model using mixed precision
model = tf.keras.Sequential([
    tf.keras.layers.Dense(64, activation='relu'),
    tf.keras.layers.Dense(10, activation='softmax')
])
```

```
model.compile(optimizer='adam',
loss='categorical_crossentropy',
metrics=['accuracy'])

model.fit(train_dataset, epochs=10)
```

XLA (Accelerated Linear Algebra) is another optimization technique that can significantly improve the performance of TensorFlow models. XLA is a domain-specific compiler that can optimize TensorFlow graphs for execution on different hardware platforms, including CPUs and GPUs. By optimizing the computation graph, XLA can reduce the memory usage and computation time of TensorFlow models.

To use XLA in TensorFlow, you can enable it using the tf.config.optimizer.set_jit(True) API. Here's an example:

```
import tensorflow as tf

# Enable XLA optimization
tf.config.optimizer.set_jit(True)

# Build and train a model using XLA optimization
model = tf.keras.Sequential([
    tf.keras.layers.Dense(64, activation='relu'),
    tf.keras.layers.Dense(10, activation='softmax')
])

model.compile(optimizer='adam',
              loss='categorical_crossentropy',
              metrics=['accuracy'])

model.fit(train_dataset, epochs=10)
```

In addition to mixed precision training and XLA, TensorFlow also provides other performance optimizations, such as data parallelism and model parallelism, which can be used to scale up the training of large models across multiple devices or machines.

## 4.17   What is TensorFlow.js, and how can you use it to deploy machine learning models in web applications?

TensorFlow.js is an open-source JavaScript library developed by Google that allows you to train, test, and deploy machine learning models in web browsers or Node.js. With TensorFlow.js, you can run pre-trained models or create and train custom models directly in the browser, without needing to install any additional software.

One of the key benefits of using TensorFlow.js is that it provides a high-level API that abstracts away the complexities of building and training machine learning models. This makes it easy for web developers to integrate machine learning into their applications, without needing to have a deep understanding of machine learning algorithms.

Some of the key features of TensorFlow.js include:

Ability to load pre-trained models: TensorFlow.js supports loading pre-trained models that have been created using TensorFlow or other frameworks. This means you can leverage existing models to perform tasks such as image recognition or natural language processing.

Training models in the browser: TensorFlow.js provides a high-level API for building and training machine learning models directly in the browser. This is useful for scenarios where you need to train models on user data or perform online learning.

Support for hardware acceleration: TensorFlow.js supports running models on both CPU and GPU, and it also provides support for WebGL, which allows you to accelerate computation using the graphics card.

Integration with web frameworks: TensorFlow.js provides integration with popular web frameworks such as React, Vue, and Angular, making it easy to add machine learning capabilities to your web applications.

Here is an example of how to use TensorFlow.js to load a pre-trained model and perform image recognition:

```
// Load the model
const model = await tf.loadLayersModel('path/to/model.json');

// Get a reference to the image element
const img = document.getElementById('myImage');

// Preprocess the image
const tensor = tf.browser.fromPixels(img)
.resizeNearestNeighbor([224, 224])
.toFloat()
.sub(meanImageNetRGB)
.div(stdImageNetRGB)
.expandDims();
```

```
// Make a prediction
const predictions = model.predict(tensor);

// Print the top 3 predictions
const top3 = Array.from(predictions.dataSync())
.map((p, i) => {
   return {
      probability: p,
      className: IMAGENET_CLASSES[i]
   };
})
.sort((a, b) => b.probability - a.probability)
.slice(0, 3);

console.log('Top 3 predictions:', top3);
```

In this example, we first load a pre-trained model using the tf.load-LayersModel function. We then get a reference to an image element on the page, and preprocess it using various operations such as resizing and normalization. Finally, we use the predict method of the model to make a prediction on the input image, and display the top 3 predictions.

## 4.18   Can you explain the concept of reinforcement learning in TensorFlow, and how to implement it using TensorFlow Agents?

Reinforcement learning (RL) is a type of machine learning that focuses on training agents to make decisions by interacting with an environment. In reinforcement learning, an agent learns to take actions in an environment to maximize a cumulative reward signal. TensorFlow offers TensorFlow Agents, a library for building and training RL agents.

The TensorFlow Agents library provides a set of pre-built RL algorithms, including Deep Q-Networks (DQN), Proximal Policy Optimization (PPO), and others. These algorithms can be used to train agents for a wide range of tasks, such as playing games or controlling robots.

To implement reinforcement learning using TensorFlow Agents, the following steps are typically taken:

Define the environment: An environment is a simulation or real-world system that an agent interacts with. It provides the agent with observations, and the agent takes actions in the environment based on those observations. In TensorFlow Agents, an environment is represented as a Python class that implements the OpenAI Gym interface.

Define the agent: An agent is a machine learning model that takes in observations from the environment and outputs actions. In TensorFlow Agents, an agent is represented as a Python class that extends the tf_agents.agents.TFAgent base class.

Define the training process: The training process involves repeatedly interacting with the environment and updating the agent's parameters based on the observed rewards. In TensorFlow Agents, the training process is typically implemented using the tf_agents.trainers.Trainer class, which provides a set of pre-built training loops.

Run the training process: The training process can be run using the tf_agents.train.utils.train_utils function, which takes as input the environment, the agent, and the trainer.

Once the agent is trained, it can be used to make decisions in new environments by simply feeding in observations and receiving actions as output.

Overall, reinforcement learning using TensorFlow Agents provides a powerful framework for building and training intelligent agents that can interact with complex environments and make decisions based on learned policies.

## 4.19   What are some advanced techniques for optimizing hyperparameters in TensorFlow, such as Bayesian optimization or genetic algorithms?

In machine learning, hyperparameters are parameters that cannot be learned directly from the training data, but rather must be set by

the practitioner before training. Optimizing hyperparameters is an
important step in building accurate and effective machine learning
models. TensorFlow offers several advanced techniques for optimizing hyperparameters, including Bayesian optimization and genetic
algorithms.

Bayesian optimization is a technique that uses Bayesian inference to
construct a probabilistic model of the objective function (i.e., the
evaluation metric that is being optimized), and then uses this model
to determine the next set of hyperparameters to try. This allows the
optimization process to be more efficient and effective, as the algorithm can intelligently select hyperparameters that are more likely to
result in good performance.

TensorFlow offers several libraries for performing Bayesian optimization, including scikit-optimize, hyperopt, and Tune. For example,
using the hyperopt library, we can define a hyperparameter space to
search over and a function to evaluate the model's performance, and
then use the fmin function to perform the optimization:

```python
from hyperopt import fmin, tpe, hp
from tensorflow.keras import layers, models

def build_model(hp):
    model = models.Sequential()
    model.add(layers.Conv2D(hp['filters'], kernel_size=3, activation=
        'relu', input_shape=(28, 28, 1)))
    model.add(layers.MaxPooling2D())
    model.add(layers.Flatten())
    model.add(layers.Dense(hp['units'], activation='relu'))
    model.add(layers.Dense(10, activation='softmax'))
    model.compile(optimizer='adam', loss='categorical_crossentropy',
        metrics=['accuracy'])
    return model

def objective(hp):
    model = build_model(hp)
    history = model.fit(train_images, train_labels, epochs=5,
        validation_split=0.2)
    return -history.history['val_accuracy'][-1]

space = {
    'filters': hp.choice('filters', [16, 32, 64]),
    'units': hp.choice('units', [64, 128, 256])
}

best = fmin(objective, space, algo=tpe.suggest, max_evals=10)
```

Genetic algorithms are another technique for optimizing hyperparameters that is inspired by natural selection. In a genetic algorithm, a
population of candidate solutions is iteratively evolved using genetic

operators such as mutation, crossover, and selection. This process gradually produces better and better solutions over time.

TensorFlow offers several libraries for performing genetic algorithms, including DEAP and TensorFlow Genetic. For example, using the TensorFlow Genetic library, we can define a population of candidate solutions and a fitness function to evaluate their performance, and then use the evolve function to perform the optimization:

```
import tensorflow as tf
import numpy as np
from tensorflow_genetic import geneticalgorithm

def build_model(params):
    model = tf.keras.Sequential()
    model.add(tf.keras.layers.Dense(params['units'], activation=
        params['activation'], input_shape=(10,)))
    model.add(tf.keras.layers.Dense(1, activation='sigmoid'))
    model.compile(optimizer=params['optimizer'], loss=params['loss'])
    return model

def fitness_func(model):
    predictions = model.predict(test_data)
    accuracy = np.mean((predictions > 0.5) == test_labels)
    return accuracy

param_definitions = {
    'units': {'type': 'int', 'min': 8, 'max': 128},
    'activation': {'type': 'choice', 'values': ['relu', 'sigmoid', '
        tanh']},
    'optimizer': {'type': 'choice', 'values': ['adam', 'sgd', '
        rmsprop']},
}
```

## 4.20   How do you implement GANs (Generative Adversarial Networks) in TensorFlow, and what are their applications?

Generative Adversarial Networks (GANs) are a type of deep learning model that can generate realistic samples in a given distribution. The model is composed of two networks: a generator that creates new data samples, and a discriminator that evaluates the authenticity of the generated samples. The two networks are trained together in an adversarial manner, with the generator trying to fool the discriminator, and the discriminator trying to distinguish between real and fake samples.

In TensorFlow, GANs can be implemented using the tf.keras API.
Here is a simple example of a GAN that generates images of handwritten digits:

```
# Generator network
generator = tf.keras.Sequential([
    tf.keras.layers.Dense(7*7*256, input_shape=(100,), use_bias=False
        ),
    tf.keras.layers.BatchNormalization(),
    tf.keras.layers.LeakyReLU(),
    tf.keras.layers.Reshape((7, 7, 256)),
    tf.keras.layers.Conv2DTranspose(128, (5, 5), strides=(1, 1),
        padding='same', use_bias=False),
    tf.keras.layers.BatchNormalization(),
    tf.keras.layers.LeakyReLU(),
    tf.keras.layers.Conv2DTranspose(64, (5, 5), strides=(2, 2),
        padding='same', use_bias=False),
    tf.keras.layers.BatchNormalization(),
    tf.keras.layers.LeakyReLU(),
    tf.keras.layers.Conv2DTranspose(1, (5, 5), strides=(2, 2),
        padding='same', use_bias=False, activation='tanh')
])

# Discriminator network
discriminator = tf.keras.Sequential([
    tf.keras.layers.Conv2D(64, (5, 5), strides=(2, 2), padding='same'
        , input_shape=[28, 28, 1]),
    tf.keras.layers.LeakyReLU(),
    tf.keras.layers.Dropout(0.3),
    tf.keras.layers.Conv2D(128, (5, 5), strides=(2, 2), padding='same
        '),
    tf.keras.layers.LeakyReLU(),
    tf.keras.layers.Dropout(0.3),
    tf.keras.layers.Flatten(),
    tf.keras.layers.Dense(1)
])

# Loss functions and optimizers
cross_entropy = tf.keras.losses.BinaryCrossentropy(from_logits=True)
generator_optimizer = tf.keras.optimizers.Adam(1e-4)
discriminator_optimizer = tf.keras.optimizers.Adam(1e-4)

# Training loop
@tf.function
def train_step(images):
    noise = tf.random.normal([BATCH_SIZE, 100])

    with tf.GradientTape() as gen_tape, tf.GradientTape() as
        disc_tape:
        generated_images = generator(noise, training=True)

        real_output = discriminator(images, training=True)
        fake_output = discriminator(generated_images, training=True)

        gen_loss = cross_entropy(tf.ones_like(fake_output), fake_output)
        disc_loss = cross_entropy(tf.ones_like(real_output), real_output)
            + cross_entropy(tf.zeros_like(fake_output), fake_output)

    gradients_of_generator = gen_tape.gradient(gen_loss, generator.
```

```
        trainable_variables)
gradients_of_discriminator = disc_tape.gradient(disc_loss,
    discriminator.trainable_variables)

generator_optimizer.apply_gradients(zip(gradients_of_generator,
    generator.trainable_variables))
discriminator_optimizer.apply_gradients(zip(
    gradients_of_discriminator, discriminator.
    trainable_variables))
```

# Chapter 5

# Expert

## 5.1 How does TensorFlow's dynamic computation graph (eager execution) compare to static computation graphs, and what are the trade-offs?

TensorFlow provides two ways to build and execute a computational graph, static computation graphs (Graph mode) and dynamic computation graphs (Eager execution). In the Graph mode, users define a computation graph before the execution and feed data into the graph to perform the computation. On the other hand, Eager execution allows users to execute operations immediately as they are called, enabling a more flexible and intuitive way to build models.

Here are some of the main differences between static and dynamic computation graphs:

Graph mode (static computation graph): In this mode, the user defines the graph structure in advance and then feeds the data into the graph to perform the computation. TensorFlow then optimizes the graph and executes it efficiently. The static graph mode is very useful when dealing with large models, especially when training on large datasets since it can be optimized for distributed execution.

Eager execution (dynamic computation graph): In this mode, the user builds the graph on the fly as they write the code. The execution is immediate, allowing the user to iterate quickly on the model and debug the code more easily. However, eager execution is slower than the static graph mode, and it cannot be as efficiently parallelized.

Here are some of the benefits and limitations of using TensorFlow's eager execution mode:

Benefits:

Eager execution allows for easier model development and debugging, as the user can run and debug each operation immediately.

Eager execution makes it easier to work with control flow operations, such as loops and conditionals.

Eager execution allows the use of Python flow control, which can make it easier to implement complex models.

Eager execution is more intuitive and easier to learn for users who are new to TensorFlow.

Limitations:

Eager execution can be slower than the static graph mode because it does not optimize the graph before execution.

Eager execution does not support distributed execution and cannot take advantage of the performance optimizations that come with distributed computing.

Eager execution can consume more memory than static graph mode because it does not perform optimizations such as constant folding.

In conclusion, the choice of whether to use the static graph mode or eager execution depends on the requirements of the project. If the model is large, and training is performed on large datasets, static computation graphs are recommended. On the other hand, if the model is small, and debugging is required, eager execution is a good choice.

## 5.2    Can you explain how the TensorFlow Profiler works and how it can be used to analyze and optimize model performance?

The TensorFlow Profiler is a tool for analyzing and optimizing the performance of TensorFlow models. It allows developers to track and visualize the execution of TensorFlow graphs, identify performance bottlenecks, and optimize the performance of their models.

The Profiler provides several different types of profiling data, including compute time, memory usage, and communication time for distributed models. It also provides a timeline view that shows the execution of each operation in the graph, as well as a graph view that displays the structure of the TensorFlow graph.

To use the Profiler, developers can add profiling hooks to their TensorFlow code, which will record profiling data during execution. For example, the following code snippet adds a profiling hook to a TensorFlow session:

```
from tensorflow.python.client import timeline

run_metadata = tf.RunMetadata()
opts = tf.profiler.ProfileOptionBuilder.float_operation()

with tf.Session() as sess:
  # Add the profiling hook
  sess.run(train_op, options=tf.RunOptions(
    trace_level=tf.RunOptions.FULL_TRACE),
    run_metadata=run_metadata)

# Retrieve the profiling data and visualize it with TensorBoard
fetched_timeline = timeline.Timeline(
  run_metadata.step_stats)
chrome_trace = fetched_timeline.generate_chrome_trace_format()
with open('timeline.json', 'w') as f:
  f.write(chrome_trace)
```

This code adds a profiling hook to a TensorFlow session and then uses the TensorFlow timeline module to generate a JSON file containing the profiling data. This file can then be visualized in the TensorFlow Profiler or in other tools such as Chrome's Trace Viewer.

By analyzing the profiling data provided by the TensorFlow Profiler, developers can identify performance bottlenecks in their models and optimize them for improved performance. For example, they may choose to adjust the batch size, modify the model architecture, or use different optimization techniques to achieve better results.

## 5.3   How do you handle large-scale, out-of-memory datasets in TensorFlow, and what are the best practices for efficient data loading and processing?

Handling large-scale, out-of-memory datasets is a common challenge in machine learning, and TensorFlow provides several tools and techniques to address this issue. Here are some best practices for efficient data loading and processing in TensorFlow:

Use tf.data API: TensorFlow's tf.data API provides an efficient way to load and preprocess large datasets. It allows you to create a pipeline of operations that can be applied to the data in parallel, such as shuffling, batching, and prefetching. Using the tf.data API can significantly improve the efficiency of data loading and processing.

Example:
```
dataset = tf.data.Dataset.from_tensor_slices((x_train, y_train))
dataset = dataset.shuffle(buffer_size=10000).batch(32).prefetch(1)
```

Use data generators: If your dataset is too large to fit in memory, you can use data generators to load the data in batches. A data generator is a function that yields batches of data from the disk or memory. This can be done using Python's built-in generators or with third-party libraries like TensorFlow's tf.keras.utils.Sequence.

Example:
```
def data_generator(data_path, batch_size):
    while True:
        data = load_data_from_disk(data_path)
        for i in range(0, len(data), batch_size):
            batch = data[i:i + batch_size]
            yield preprocess_data(batch)
```

Use distributed training: If you have access to a cluster of machines, you can use distributed training to speed up the training process.

TensorFlow provides several strategies for distributed training, such as parameter server and all-reduce.

Example:

```
strategy = tf.distribute.experimental.MultiWorkerMirroredStrategy()
with strategy.scope():
   model = create_model()
model.compile(optimizer='adam', loss='binary_crossentropy', metrics
   =['accuracy'])
model.fit(dataset, epochs=10)
```

Use on-the-fly data augmentation: Instead of pre-processing the entire dataset, you can use on-the-fly data augmentation to generate new samples on the fly during training. This can help increase the size of the dataset and improve the generalization of the model.

Example:

```
data_augmentation = tf.keras.Sequential([
   tf.keras.layers.experimental.preprocessing.RandomFlip("
      horizontal_and_vertical"),
   tf.keras.layers.experimental.preprocessing.RandomRotation(0.2),
   tf.keras.layers.experimental.preprocessing.RandomZoom(0.1),
])
model = tf.keras.Sequential([
   data_augmentation,
   tf.keras.layers.Conv2D(32, (3,3), activation='relu'),
   tf.keras.layers.MaxPooling2D(pool_size=(2,2)),
   ...
])
```

Use data compression: If your dataset is too large to fit on disk, you can use data compression techniques such as gzip or Blosc to reduce the size of the data. This can help speed up the data loading process and reduce the amount of disk space needed to store the data.

Example:

```
# Save compressed data to disk
with tf.io.gfile.GFile('data.gz', 'wb') as f:
   f.write(tf.io.gfile.GFile('data', 'rb').read())
# Load compressed data from disk
with tf.io.gfile.GFile('data.gz', 'rb') as f:
   data = f.read()
   data = gzip.decompress(data)
```

By following these best practices, you can efficiently handle large-scale, out-of-memory datasets in TensorFlow and train machine learning models on large datasets.

# 5.4    How can you implement unsupervised pre-training techniques, such as self-supervised learning or contrastive learning, in TensorFlow?

Unsupervised pre-training techniques are used to train deep neural networks using unlabelled data. Two popular unsupervised pre-training techniques are self-supervised learning and contrastive learning. TensorFlow provides several APIs to implement these techniques.

Self-Supervised Learning

Self-supervised learning is a type of unsupervised learning where the network learns to predict missing parts of an input data. This is done by removing a part of the input data and training the network to predict that missing part. For example, in image processing, a part of an image can be removed, and the network is trained to predict that missing part.

The following code snippet shows how to implement a self-supervised learning model using TensorFlow:

```
import tensorflow as tf
from tensorflow import keras
from tensorflow.keras import layers

# Define a model with a masked language modeling head
inputs = keras.Input(shape=(32, 32, 3))
x = layers.Conv2D(64, 3, activation="relu")(inputs)
x = layers.Conv2D(64, 3, activation="relu")(x)
x = layers.MaxPooling2D(2)(x)
x = layers.Conv2D(128, 3, activation="relu")(x)
x = layers.Conv2D(128, 3, activation="relu")(x)
x = layers.MaxPooling2D(2)(x)
x = layers.Flatten()(x)
x = layers.Dense(256, activation="relu")(x)
x = layers.Dropout(0.5)(x)
outputs = layers.Dense(128)(x)
model = keras.Model(inputs=inputs, outputs=outputs, name="
    self_supervised_model")

# Compile the model
model.compile(optimizer=keras.optimizers.Adam(learning_rate=1e-4))

# Train the model on a dataset with missing parts
dataset = tf.data.Dataset.from_tensor_slices((x_train, x_train)) #
    Use x_train as both input and target
dataset = dataset.shuffle(buffer_size=1024).batch(64)
model.fit(dataset, epochs=10)
```

In this example, a self-supervised learning model is defined with a masked language modeling head. The model is trained on a dataset with missing parts, where x_train is used as both the input and target.

Contrastive Learning

Contrastive learning is a type of unsupervised learning where the network learns to map similar inputs to nearby points in the embedding space and dissimilar inputs to distant points in the embedding space. This is done by training the network to maximize the similarity between the representations of similar inputs and minimize the similarity between the representations of dissimilar inputs.

The following code snippet shows how to implement a contrastive learning model using TensorFlow:

```
import tensorflow as tf
from tensorflow import keras
from tensorflow.keras import layers

# Define a model with a contrastive loss
inputs = keras.Input(shape=(32, 32, 3))
x = layers.Conv2D(64, 3, activation="relu")(inputs)
x = layers.Conv2D(64, 3, activation="relu")(x)
x = layers.MaxPooling2D(2)(x)
x = layers.Conv2D(128, 3, activation="relu")(x)
x = layers.Conv2D(128, 3, activation="relu")(x)
x = layers.MaxPooling2D(2)(x)
x = layers.Flatten()(x)
x = layers.Dense(256, activation="relu")(x)
outputs = layers.Dense(128)(x)
model = keras.Model(inputs=inputs, outputs=outputs, name="
    contrastive_model")

# Define the contrastive loss function
def contrastive_loss(y_true, y_pred):
  margin =
  ...
```

## 5.5    What are some advanced optimization techniques in TensorFlow, such as second-order optimization methods or natural gradient descent?

In machine learning, optimization techniques are used to find the values of model parameters that minimize a loss function. TensorFlow offers various optimization techniques, including advanced ones, that can be used to train deep learning models.

Here are some examples of advanced optimization techniques in TensorFlow:

Second-order optimization methods: These methods use second-order derivatives of the loss function to compute the direction of parameter updates. Examples of second-order optimization methods include the Hessian-free optimization algorithm, the L-BFGS algorithm, and the conjugate gradient algorithm. TensorFlow provides an implementation of the L-BFGS algorithm in the tf.train.Optimizer class.

Natural gradient descent: This optimization technique uses the Fisher information matrix to compute the direction of parameter updates. Natural gradient descent is based on the idea that the distance between two probability distributions should be measured using the Kullback-Leibler divergence, rather than the Euclidean distance. TensorFlow provides an implementation of natural gradient descent in the tf.train.ProximalAdagradOptimizer class.

Adversarial training: This optimization technique involves training a model to generate adversarial examples, which are input samples that are deliberately designed to mislead the model. By training the model to be robust to adversarial examples, the model can be made more generalizable and robust to noise in the data. TensorFlow provides an implementation of adversarial training in the tf adversarial module.

Curriculum learning: This optimization technique involves training a model on a series of progressively more difficult tasks or samples. By gradually increasing the difficulty of the training data, the model can learn to generalize better and avoid overfitting. TensorFlow provides an implementation of curriculum learning in the tf.contrib.training module.

Ensemble methods: Ensemble methods involve training multiple models and combining their predictions to improve performance. Examples of ensemble methods include bagging, boosting, and stacking. TensorFlow provides an implementation of ensemble methods in the tf.estimator API.

Overall, these advanced optimization techniques can help to improve the accuracy and robustness of deep learning models in TensorFlow. However, they can also be more computationally expensive and harder to implement than simpler optimization techniques, so they should be used judiciously based on the specific needs of the task at hand.

## 5.6 How can you use TensorFlow's low-level APIs to build custom training loops, gradient calculations, and other advanced functionalities?

TensorFlow provides both high-level and low-level APIs to build and train machine learning models. While the high-level APIs, such as Keras and Estimators, offer a more user-friendly and streamlined approach to building models, the low-level APIs provide more flexibility and control over the training process. In this answer, we will discuss how to use TensorFlow's low-level APIs to build custom training loops, gradient calculations, and other advanced functionalities.

The low-level APIs in TensorFlow are centered around the concept of a computational graph, which represents the mathematical operations that make up a machine learning model. A computational graph is a directed acyclic graph (DAG) that consists of nodes and edges, where nodes represent mathematical operations and edges represent the flow of data between nodes. TensorFlow's low-level APIs allow developers to define and manipulate this computational graph directly.

To build a custom training loop using TensorFlow's low-level APIs, we first need to define the computational graph that represents our model. We can do this using the tf.placeholder and tf.Variable operations to create placeholders for the input data and variables for the model parameters. We can then define the mathematical operations that make up our model using operations such as tf.matmul and tf.nn.relu. Once we have defined the computational graph for our model, we can use the tf.gradients operation to compute the gradients of the loss function with respect to the model parameters.

With the computational graph defined, we can then use a loop to iterate over the training data and perform the forward and backward passes of the model. In each iteration, we feed a batch of training data into the placeholders using the feed_dict argument, and then use the session.run method to compute the forward pass and gradients of the loss function. We can then use an optimization algorithm such as gradient descent to update the model parameters based on the computed gradients.

Here is an example of how to build a custom training loop for a simple linear regression model using TensorFlow's low-level APIs:

```
import tensorflow as tf
import numpy as np

# Define the computational graph for the linear regression model
x = tf.placeholder(tf.float32, shape=[None, 1])
y_true = tf.placeholder(tf.float32, shape=[None, 1])
w = tf.Variable(tf.zeros([1, 1]))
b = tf.Variable(tf.zeros([1]))
y_pred = tf.matmul(x, w) + b
loss = tf.reduce_mean(tf.square(y_true - y_pred))

# Define the optimization algorithm
learning_rate = 0.01
optimizer = tf.train.GradientDescentOptimizer(learning_rate)
grads_and_vars = optimizer.compute_gradients(loss)
train_op = optimizer.apply_gradients(grads_and_vars)

# Generate some random training data
np.random.seed(0)
x_train = np.random.randn(100, 1)
y_train = 2 * x_train + 1 + np.random.randn(100, 1) * 0.1

# Train the model using a custom training loop
num_epochs = 100
batch_size = 10
num_batches = x_train.shape[0] // batch_size

with tf.Session() as sess:
    sess.run(tf.global_variables_initializer())

    for epoch in range(num_epochs):
        epoch_loss = 0.0

        for i in range(num_batches):
            start_idx = i * batch_size
```

```
        end_idx = (i + 1) * batch_size
        batch_x = x_train[start_idx:end_idx]
        batch_y = y_train[start_idx:end_idx]

        _, batch_loss = sess.run([train_op, loss], feed_dict={x:
            batch_x, y_true: batch_y})
        epoch_loss += batch_loss

    epoch_loss /= num_batches
    print
...
```

## 5.7    What are the key principles of Capsule Networks, and how can you implement them using TensorFlow?

Capsule Networks are a type of neural network that aim to overcome the limitations of Convolutional Neural Networks (CNNs) in handling spatial hierarchies and transformations. They were first introduced by Hinton et al. in 2011 and have since shown promising results in various tasks such as image classification, object detection, and video analysis.

The main idea behind Capsule Networks is to use groups of neurons, called capsules, to represent visual concepts such as objects or parts of objects. Each capsule consists of a vector of scalar activations, which represents the probability of the existence of the corresponding concept and its pose parameters such as position, orientation, and scale. These pose parameters are learned during training and allow the capsules to model spatial relationships and transformations between objects and parts.

The key principles of Capsule Networks can be summarized as follows:

Dynamic routing: Capsules communicate with each other through a dynamic routing mechanism, which enables them to share information about their pose and agreement with other capsules in the same layer. This allows the network to model higher-level concepts and relationships between objects and parts.

Margin loss: Capsule Networks use a margin loss function to encourage the network to learn discriminative and robust representations of the input data. The margin loss penalizes the network if the probability of the correct label is lower than a margin, while also penalizing if the probability of incorrect labels is higher than a margin.

Reconstruction loss: Capsule Networks also use a reconstruction loss to encourage the network to learn meaningful representations of the input data. The reconstruction loss is calculated by comparing the output of the network to a reconstruction of the input data, which is generated from the pose parameters of the capsules. This helps the network to learn more informative and invariant representations of the input data.

To implement Capsule Networks in TensorFlow, we can use the tf.keras API and define custom layers and loss functions. Here is an example implementation of a Capsule Network for image classification:

```
import tensorflow as tf
from tensorflow.keras.layers import Conv2D, Dense, Flatten, Reshape

class CapsuleLayer(tf.keras.layers.Layer):
    def __init__(self, num_capsules, capsule_dim, routings=3, **
        kwargs):
        super(CapsuleLayer, self).__init__(**kwargs)
        self.num_capsules = num_capsules
        self.capsule_dim = capsule_dim
        self.routings = routings

    def build(self, input_shape):
        _, h, w, c = input_shape
        self.conv = Conv2D(self.num_capsules * self.capsule_dim,
        kernel_size=3,
        strides=1,
        padding='same',
        activation='relu')
        self.pose = Dense(self.num_capsules * self.capsule_dim)
        self.activation = Dense(self.num_capsules, activation='softmax
            ')

    def call(self, inputs):
        conv_output = self.conv(inputs)
        _, h, w, c = conv_output.shape
        capsules = tf.reshape(conv_output, [-1, h * w * self.
            num_capsules, self.capsule_dim])
        poses = self.pose(capsules)
        activations = self.activation(poses)
        for i in range(self.routings):
            route_probs = tf.nn.softmax(activations, axis=1)
            route_probs = tf.expand_dims(route_probs, axis=-1)
            weighted_capsules = route_probs * capsules
            weighted_sum = tf.reduce_sum(weighted_capsules, axis=1)
            capsules = self.squash(weighted_sum)
            if i < self.routings - 1:
                poses = self.pose(capsules)
                activations = tf.reduce_sum(poses * capsules, axis=-1
    ...
```

# 5.8 How do you perform multi-modal learning in TensorFlow, and what are its applications?

Multi-modal learning is a type of machine learning that involves training models on multiple types of data inputs or "modalities," such as images, text, and audio. The goal is to learn relationships between the different modalities, enabling the model to make predictions based on inputs from multiple sources.

In TensorFlow, there are several approaches to performing multi-modal learning, including:

Fusion-based approaches: These approaches involve merging the outputs from different modalities using techniques such as concatenation, addition, or multiplication. The merged output is then fed into a neural network for further processing.

Cross-modal approaches: These approaches involve learning separate representations for each modality, then training a joint model that can effectively combine them. This can be done using techniques such as cross-modal retrieval or multi-task learning.

Graph-based approaches: These approaches involve representing the relationships between different modalities as a graph, and using graph-based neural networks to learn the relationships. This can be particularly useful for tasks such as knowledge graph construction or link prediction.

Here's an example of how to implement a fusion-based approach to multi-modal learning using TensorFlow:

```
import tensorflow as tf

# Define two input modalities
image_input = tf.keras.layers.Input(shape=(224, 224, 3))
text_input = tf.keras.layers.Input(shape=(100,))

# Define separate processing pipelines for each modality
image_pipeline = tf.keras.Sequential([
    tf.keras.layers.Conv2D(32, (3, 3), activation='relu'),
    tf.keras.layers.MaxPooling2D((2, 2)),
    tf.keras.layers.Flatten()
])(image_input)

text_pipeline = tf.keras.Sequential([
```

```
    tf.keras.layers.Embedding(input_dim=1000, output_dim=64),
    tf.keras.layers.LSTM(32)
])(text_input)

# Merge the output from each pipeline using concatenation
merged = tf.keras.layers.concatenate([image_pipeline, text_pipeline
    ])

# Add some dense layers for further processing
merged = tf.keras.layers.Dense(64, activation='relu')(merged)
merged = tf.keras.layers.Dense(32, activation='relu')(merged)

# Define the output layer for the joint model
output = tf.keras.layers.Dense(1, activation='sigmoid')(merged)

# Define the joint model
model = tf.keras.models.Model(inputs=[image_input, text_input],
    outputs=output)
```

In this example, we define two separate processing pipelines for images and text, then merge their outputs using concatenation. We then add some additional dense layers for further processing, before defining the final output layer for the joint model. Finally, we define the joint model using the tf.keras.models.Model API, specifying both input modalities and the output.

## 5.9    Can you explain the concept of meta-learning in TensorFlow, and how it can be used to improve model generalization?

Meta-learning, also known as "learning to learn," is a subfield of machine learning that aims to enable models to quickly adapt to new tasks with few examples by leveraging prior knowledge acquired from similar tasks. In other words, meta-learning is about learning how to learn.

The key idea behind meta-learning is to train a model on a set of tasks, such that it learns to generalize across tasks and becomes more capable of adapting to new tasks. This can be done by defining a meta-objective that measures how well the model is able to learn from a given task, and using this objective to optimize the model's learning algorithm.

One common approach to meta-learning is to use a variation of gradient-based optimization called "meta-gradient descent." In this approach, the model is trained to update its weights in a way that minimizes the loss on a set of tasks, while also learning how to update its weights more efficiently based on the gradients computed during this process. This allows the model to quickly adapt to new tasks with few examples, by using the knowledge it has gained from previous tasks.

In TensorFlow, meta-learning can be implemented using a variety of techniques, such as:

Model-agnostic meta-learning (MAML): MAML is a popular approach to meta-learning that can be applied to any differentiable model. It involves training the model on a set of tasks, and then using the gradients of the model's parameters with respect to the task-specific losses to update the parameters in a way that improves its generalization to new tasks.

Reptile: Reptile is another approach to meta-learning that is similar to MAML, but uses a simpler optimization procedure. Instead of directly optimizing the model's parameters, Reptile updates a set of "fast weights" that are used to initialize the model's parameters for each new task. The fast weights are then updated based on the gradients of the model's parameters with respect to the task-specific losses.

Meta-learning with memory-augmented neural networks: This approach involves augmenting the model with an external memory module that can store information about previous tasks. The model is trained to read from and write to this memory module in order to quickly adapt to new tasks.

Meta-learning has many applications in areas such as computer vision, natural language processing, and robotics, where models often need to quickly adapt to new tasks or environments. It can be used to improve the generalization and efficiency of models, and to enable models to learn from less data than would be required by traditional machine learning approaches.

## 5.10 How can you use TensorFlow with hardware accelerators, such as GPUs, TPUs, and FPGAs, for maximum performance?

TensorFlow is designed to work seamlessly with a variety of hardware accelerators, including GPUs, TPUs, and FPGAs, to speed up the training and inference of machine learning models. In this answer, we will discuss how to use TensorFlow with these hardware accelerators.

GPUs

GPUs (Graphics Processing Units) are widely used for accelerating deep learning workloads due to their high computational power and ability to perform parallel computations. TensorFlow supports GPUs through its CUDA and cuDNN libraries, which enable efficient GPU computation.

To use TensorFlow with GPUs, you need to ensure that you have installed the necessary drivers and libraries for your GPU. TensorFlow provides pre-built binaries that support GPU acceleration for popular GPU architectures, including NVIDIA GPUs. Once you have installed the appropriate drivers and libraries, you can use TensorFlow with GPUs by specifying the device placement of operations using the tf.device context manager. For example, to use a GPU for matrix multiplication, you can write:

```
import tensorflow as tf

with tf.device('/GPU:0'):
    a = tf.constant([[1., 2.], [3., 4.]])
    b = tf.constant([[5., 6.], [7., 8.]])
    c = tf.matmul(a, b)
```

This will ensure that the matrix multiplication operation is executed on the GPU. TensorFlow will automatically select the GPU with the lowest memory usage by default.

TPUs

TPUs (Tensor Processing Units) are specialized hardware accelerators designed by Google for deep learning workloads. TPUs are particularly useful for large-scale training tasks, as they can acceler-

ate training by several orders of magnitude compared to CPUs and
GPUs.

To use TPUs with TensorFlow, you need to ensure that you have
access to a TPU device and that you have installed the necessary
software components, including the Cloud TPU client library. Once
you have access to a TPU device, you can use it with TensorFlow by
specifying the TPU device as the execution target. For example:

```
import tensorflow as tf

resolver = tf.distribute.cluster_resolver.TPUClusterResolver(tpu='
    grpc://10.240.1.2:8470')
tf.config.experimental_connect_to_cluster(resolver)
tf.tpu.experimental.initialize_tpu_system(resolver)
strategy = tf.distribute.TPUStrategy(resolver)

with strategy.scope():
    model = tf.keras.Sequential([...])

    model.compile(optimizer=tf.keras.optimizers.Adam(),
        loss=tf.keras.losses.BinaryCrossentropy(),
        metrics=[tf.keras.metrics.BinaryAccuracy()])

    model.fit(train_dataset, epochs=10, steps_per_epoch=200)
```

This will ensure that the model is executed on the TPU device.

FPGAs

FPGAs (Field-Programmable Gate Arrays) are programmable hardware devices that can be configured to perform specific computations.
FPGAs are particularly useful for specialized deep learning workloads,
as they can be customized to accelerate specific operations.

To use FPGAs with TensorFlow, you need to ensure that you have
access to an FPGA device and that you have installed the necessary
software components, including the FPGA SDK. Once you have access to an FPGA device, you can use it with TensorFlow by defining
custom operations that are optimized for FPGA acceleration. TensorFlow provides an API for defining custom operations using the
tf.function decorator. For example:

```
import tensorflow as tf

@tf.function
def my_fpga_op(x, y):
    # Define custom FPGA operation here
    return result

x = tf.constant([1, 2, 3])
```

```
y = tf.constant([4, 5, 6])
result = my_fpga_op(x, y)
```

This will ensure that the custom operation is executed on the FPGA
device.

## 5.11   What are the main differences between TensorFlow's graph and non-graph modes, and how can you utilize them effectively?

TensorFlow offers two modes of execution, the Graph mode, and the
Eager mode. The main difference between these two modes is the
way they build and execute the computational graph.

In Graph mode, the user first defines a static computational graph
that represents the operations and data dependencies of the model.
The graph is then compiled and optimized for execution, which allows
for efficient parallelism and distributed execution across devices and
servers. The Graph mode is the default mode in TensorFlow 1.x, and
it is still available in TensorFlow 2.x for backward compatibility.

In Eager mode, the user can execute TensorFlow operations immediately as they are called, without the need to define a static computational graph. Eager mode provides a more interactive and intuitive
programming interface, similar to other deep learning frameworks
such as PyTorch and Chainer. Eager mode also supports dynamic
control flow and Python control structures, which makes it easier to
implement custom training loops and other advanced functionalities.
Eager mode is the default mode in TensorFlow 2.x.

Here is an example of how to use both modes to build and train a
simple neural network:

```
import tensorflow as tf

# Graph mode
tf.compat.v1.disable_eager_execution()

# Define the computational graph
x = tf.compat.v1.placeholder(tf.float32, shape=(None, 784))
```

```python
y = tf.compat.v1.placeholder(tf.float32, shape=(None, 10))
w = tf.Variable(tf.random.normal((784, 10)), name='weights')
b = tf.Variable(tf.zeros((10,)), name='biases')
logits = tf.matmul(x, w) + b
loss = tf.reduce_mean(tf.nn.softmax_cross_entropy_with_logits(labels
    =y, logits=logits))
optimizer = tf.compat.v1.train.GradientDescentOptimizer(0.01).
    minimize(loss)

# Execute the graph
with tf.compat.v1.Session() as sess:
    sess.run(tf.compat.v1.global_variables_initializer())
    for i in range(1000):
        batch_x, batch_y = get_next_batch()
        sess.run(optimizer, feed_dict={x: batch_x, y: batch_y})
        if i % 100 == 0:
            print('Loss at step {}: {}'.format(i, sess.run(loss,
                feed_dict={x: batch_x, y: batch_y})))

# Eager mode
tf.compat.v1.enable_eager_execution()


# Define the model and optimizer
class SimpleModel(tf.keras.Model):
    def __init__(self):
        super(SimpleModel, self).__init__()
        self.w = tf.Variable(tf.random.normal((784, 10)), name='
            weights')
        self.b = tf.Variable(tf.zeros((10,)), name='biases')

    def call(self, inputs):
        logits = tf.matmul(inputs, self.w) + self.b
        return logits

model = SimpleModel()
optimizer = tf.keras.optimizers.SGD(0.01)

# Train the model
for i in range(1000):
    batch_x, batch_y = get_next_batch()
    with tf.GradientTape() as tape:
        logits = model(batch_x)
        loss = tf.reduce_mean(tf.nn.softmax_cross_entropy_with_logits(
            labels=batch_y, logits=logits))
    gradients = tape.gradient(loss, model.trainable_variables)
    optimizer.apply_gradients(zip(gradients, model.
        trainable_variables))
    if i % 100 == 0:
        print('Loss at step {}: {}'.format(i, loss))
```

As shown in the example, the Graph mode uses placeholders to define the input and output tensors of the model, and variables to store the model parameters. The user then defines the loss function and the optimizer, and uses a session to execute the graph and update the variables using the optimizer.

## 5.12 How do you perform active learning in TensorFlow, and what are the benefits of incorporating it into your training process?

Active learning is a type of machine learning where the algorithm interacts with a human to obtain the most relevant and informative data points for training. In other words, it is a process of selecting data samples that are the most informative for the model's training, instead of labeling all the data. This approach reduces the need for human labeling and saves time and resources.

In TensorFlow, there are different methods to implement active learning. One approach is to use uncertainty sampling, which selects the samples where the model is uncertain or has a high error rate. This approach ensures that the model is trained on the most important and informative data points. Another approach is to use diversity sampling, which selects samples that are diverse and different from the current training data, so that the model can learn from a wide range of examples.

To implement active learning in TensorFlow, one can use the TensorFlow Datasets library, which provides many pre-processed datasets with a standardized API. The library has support for splitting the dataset into training, validation, and test sets. One can then use TensorFlow's active learning modules, such as tf.data.experimental.ActiveLearningSampler, to create a sampler that selects the most informative samples for training.

Here is an example code snippet that demonstrates how to use active learning in TensorFlow using the CIFAR-10 dataset:

```
import tensorflow as tf
import tensorflow_datasets as tfds

# Load the CIFAR-10 dataset
(ds_train, ds_test), ds_info = tfds.load(
    'cifar10',
    split=['train', 'test'],
    shuffle_files=True,
    as_supervised=True,
    with_info=True,
)
```

```
# Define the model architecture
model = tf.keras.Sequential([
    tf.keras.layers.Conv2D(32, 3, activation='relu', input_shape=(32,
        32, 3)),
    tf.keras.layers.MaxPooling2D(),
    tf.keras.layers.Flatten(),
    tf.keras.layers.Dense(10)
])

# Define the loss function and optimizer
loss_fn = tf.keras.losses.SparseCategoricalCrossentropy(from_logits=
    True)
optimizer = tf.keras.optimizers.Adam()


# Define the active learning sampler
sampler = tf.data.experimental.ActiveLearningSampler(
    ds_train,
    model,
    num_samples=5000,
    initial_random_samples=1000,
    diversity_fn=None,
)

# Define the training loop
for i, (x, y) in enumerate(ds_train.take(10000)):
    # Train the model on the selected samples
    with tf.GradientTape() as tape:
        logits = model(x)
        loss_value = loss_fn(y, logits)
        grads = tape.gradient(loss_value, model.trainable_variables)
        optimizer.apply_gradients(zip(grads, model.trainable_variables
            ))

    # Update the active learning sampler with the new samples
    if i % 10 == 0:
        sampler.update(model)

    # Evaluate the model on the test set
    if i % 100 == 0:
        test_loss = tf.keras.metrics.Mean()
        test_acc = tf.keras.metrics.SparseCategoricalAccuracy()
        for x_test, y_test in ds_test:
            logits = model(x_test)
            loss_value = loss_fn(y_test, logits)
            test_loss(loss_value)
            test_acc(y_test, logits)
            print(f"Step␣{i}:␣test_loss={test_loss.result()},␣
                test_accuracy={test_acc.result()}")
```

In this example, we first load the CIFAR-10 dataset using tfds.load and define the model architecture, loss function, and optimizer. We then define an ActiveLearningSampler object with a specified number of samples and initial random samples, and use it to update the model in each iteration of the training loop. We also evaluate the model on

## 5.13 Can you explain the concept of curriculum learning, and how can you implement it in TensorFlow?

Curriculum learning is a training strategy that involves presenting the training data to the model in a structured and gradually increasing order of complexity. The idea is to start with easier examples or concepts and gradually increase the difficulty level of the training examples over time, so that the model can learn more efficiently and effectively.

The basic principle of curriculum learning is that by presenting simpler examples first, the model can develop an initial understanding of the problem at hand, and gradually build upon that understanding to learn more complex concepts. This can be particularly useful in domains where the training data is very large and diverse, and the model needs to learn from many different types of examples.

In TensorFlow, there are several ways to implement curriculum learning. One approach is to manually sort the training data into batches or subsets, based on their difficulty level, and present these to the model in a structured order during training. Another approach is to use a dynamic curriculum, where the model itself decides which examples to learn from next, based on its current performance and the difficulty level of the examples.

Here's an example of how to implement curriculum learning in TensorFlow using the dynamic approach:

```
import tensorflow as tf

# Define a custom data loader that returns examples in increasing
    order of difficulty
class DataLoader:
    def __init__(self, data):
        self.data = data
        self.cur_idx = 0

    def next_batch(self, batch_size):
        # Define a function to compute the difficulty level of each
            example
        def get_difficulty(example):
            # Compute the difficulty level based on some criteria
            return difficulty

        # Sort the remaining examples by difficulty level
        sorted_data = sorted(self.data[self.cur_idx:], key=
```

```
        get_difficulty)

    # Get the next batch of examples in the sorted order
    batch_data = sorted_data[:batch_size]

    # Update the current index
    self.cur_idx += batch_size

    return batch_data

# Define a model that uses the curriculum learning strategy
class MyModel(tf.keras.Model):
    def __init__(self):
        super(MyModel, self).__init__()
        # Define the layers and variables of the model

    def call(self, inputs):
        # Define the forward pass of the model

# Define the training loop
def train(model, data_loader, optimizer, num_epochs, batch_size):
    for epoch in range(num_epochs):
        # Initialize the loss and accuracy metrics
        total_loss = 0.0
        num_correct = 0

        # Get the next batch of examples using the data loader
        batch_data = data_loader.next_batch(batch_size)

        # Iterate over the batch of examples
        for example in batch_data:
            # Compute the model output and loss for the example
            with tf.GradientTape() as tape:
            # Compute the model output for the example
            logits = model(example['input'])
            # Compute the loss based on the output and ground truth
                labels
            loss = compute_loss(logits, example['label'])

            # Update the model variables based on the computed gradients
            grads = tape.gradient(loss, model.trainable_variables)
            optimizer.apply_gradients(zip(grads, model.trainable_variables
                ))

            # Update the loss and accuracy metrics
            total_loss += loss.numpy()
            if tf.argmax(logits).numpy() == example['label']:
            num_correct += 1

        # Compute the average loss and accuracy for the epoch
        avg_loss = total_loss / len(batch_data)
        avg_accuracy = num_correct / len(batch_data)

        # Print the metrics for the epoch
        print('Epoch {}: loss = {}, accuracy = {}'.format(epoch,
            avg_loss, avg_accuracy))

        # Initialize the data loader and model
        data_loader = DataLoader(data)
        model = MyModel()
```

## 5.14  How can you build and train spiking neural networks using TensorFlow, and what are their applications?

Spiking Neural Networks (SNNs) are a type of neural network that model the behavior of biological neurons more closely than traditional artificial neural networks.  SNNs operate using spikes or pulses of electrical activity that are transmitted between neurons, and they are able to encode information in the timing of these spikes. SNNs have been shown to be more energy-efficient and better suited for tasks such as event-based vision and time-series processing.

In TensorFlow, SNNs can be built and trained using the Spiking Neural Network (SNN) API, which is built on top of TensorFlow's core functionality. The SNN API allows users to define and simulate the behavior of spiking neurons, as well as to define the connectivity between them.

To build an SNN in TensorFlow, first, the user defines the spiking neurons and the connectivity between them. This can be done using the built-in functions and objects in the SNN API, such as the spiking_relu and SpikingConnection objects.

Once the SNN has been defined, it can be trained using backpropagation through time (BPTT), which is a type of gradient descent algorithm that works with spiking neurons. During training, the input data is presented to the network, and the network's responses are compared to the desired output using a loss function. The gradients of the loss function with respect to the network's weights are then computed using BPTT and used to update the weights.

SNNs have a wide range of applications, including event-based vision, speech recognition, and robotics. They are particularly well-suited for tasks that require processing of information in a time-dependent manner, such as predicting the next frame in a video sequence or recognizing speech.

In summary, building and training SNNs in TensorFlow involves defining the spiking neurons and connectivity between them, and then training the network using BPTT. SNNs have a wide range of applications and are particularly well-suited for time-dependent tasks.

# 5.15 What are the key principles of one-shot learning and few-shot learning, and how can you implement them using TensorFlow?

One-shot learning and few-shot learning are techniques used in machine learning to handle situations where there are limited data points available for a particular task. One-shot learning refers to the task of learning to recognize new objects with only one example per class, while few-shot learning refers to learning with a small number of examples per class.

The main idea behind these techniques is to leverage prior knowledge or structure in the data to learn better generalizations from the limited data available. This is in contrast to traditional machine learning methods that require large amounts of labeled data to learn accurate models.

In TensorFlow, one can implement one-shot and few-shot learning using various techniques, such as siamese networks, metric learning, and meta-learning. Siamese networks are a type of neural network that learns to compare two input examples and output a similarity score. They can be used for one-shot learning by training the network to recognize new objects based on a single example per class. Metric learning is a method used to learn a distance metric between data points, which can be useful for few-shot learning. Meta-learning, also known as learning to learn, is a technique used to train models that can learn new tasks with minimal or no data.

Here's an example of how to implement a siamese network in TensorFlow for one-shot learning:

```
import tensorflow as tf
from tensorflow.keras.layers import Input, Conv2D, Flatten, Dense

# Define the siamese network architecture
input_shape = (28, 28, 1)
left_input = Input(input_shape)
right_input = Input(input_shape)

convnet = Sequential([
    Conv2D(64, (3,3), activation='relu', input_shape=input_shape),
    Flatten(),
    Dense(128, activation='sigmoid')
])
```

```
# Encode the left and right input
encoded_l = convnet(left_input)
encoded_r = convnet(right_input)

# Define the distance measure used to compare the encoded inputs
L1_distance = lambda x: tf.keras.backend.abs(x[0]-x[1])
distance = Lambda(L1_distance)([encoded_l, encoded_r])

# Define the final output layer
prediction = Dense(1, activation='sigmoid')(distance)

# Create the siamese network model
siamese_net = Model(inputs=[left_input,right_input],outputs=
    prediction)

# Compile the model with binary crossentropy loss
siamese_net.compile(loss='binary_crossentropy', optimizer='adam')
```

This code defines a siamese network that takes in two inputs, left_input and right_input, and outputs a similarity score between them. The architecture consists of two identical convolutional neural networks that encode the left and right inputs, respectively. The encoded inputs are then compared using an L1 distance measure, and the final output layer produces a binary prediction (0 or 1) based on the similarity score.

To use this network for one-shot learning, we can train it on a dataset of pairs of images, where each pair contains one example of a new object and one example of a previously seen object. During training, we can adjust the network's weights to maximize the similarity score between the new and previously seen objects, while minimizing the similarity score between different new objects.

In summary, one-shot and few-shot learning are techniques used in machine learning to learn from limited data. In TensorFlow, we can implement these techniques using various methods, such as siamese networks, metric learning, and meta-learning. These techniques can be used for a variety of tasks, such as image recognition, natural language processing, and more.

## 5.16   How do you use TensorFlow's APIs to implement reinforcement learning algorithms, such as Proximal Policy Optimization (PPO) or Deep Q-Networks (DQN)?

Reinforcement learning (RL) is a type of machine learning in which an agent learns to perform actions in an environment to maximize a reward signal. TensorFlow provides several APIs to implement RL algorithms, such as Proximal Policy Optimization (PPO) and Deep Q-Networks (DQN).

The TensorFlow Agents (tf-agents) library provides a set of building blocks for creating RL agents. It includes pre-built components for implementing common RL algorithms, as well as tools for defining custom agents.

To implement PPO in TensorFlow, you can use the tf-agents library to define an actor-critic network that predicts both the policy and value function. The policy is optimized using the PPO loss function, which is a combination of the policy gradient loss and a clipped surrogate loss. The value function is optimized using the mean squared error (MSE) loss. The training process involves collecting experience by running the agent in the environment, and then using this experience to update the network parameters using backpropagation.

Here's an example of how to implement PPO in TensorFlow using the tf-agents library:

```
import tensorflow as tf
from tf_agents.environments import suite_gym
from tf_agents.networks import actor_distribution_network,
    value_network
from tf_agents.agents.ppo import ppo_agent
from tf_agents.replay_buffers import tf_uniform_replay_buffer
from tf_agents.metrics import tf_metrics
from tf_agents.drivers.dynamic_step_driver import DynamicStepDriver
from tf_agents.utils.common import function, Checkpointer

# Create the environment
env_name = 'CartPole-v0'
env = suite_gym.load(env_name)

# Define the network
fc_layer_params = (100,)
actor_net = actor_distribution_network.ActorDistributionNetwork(
```

```
      env.observation_spec(),
      env.action_spec(),
      fc_layer_params=fc_layer_params)
value_net = value_network.ValueNetwork(
      env.observation_spec(),
      fc_layer_params=fc_layer_params)


# Define the PPO agent
optimizer = tf.compat.v1.train.AdamOptimizer(learning_rate=1e-3)
train_step = tf.Variable(0)
update_period = 5
ppo = ppo_agent.PPOAgent(
      env.time_step_spec(),
      env.action_spec(),
      optimizer=optimizer,
      actor_net=actor_net,
      value_net=value_net,
      num_epochs=10,
      num_parallel_environments=1,
      train_step_counter=train_step,
      use_gae=True,
      use_td_lambda_return=True,
      normalize_rewards=True,
      normalize_observations=True,
      discount_factor=0.99,
      entropy_regularization=0.0,
      importance_ratio_clipping=0.2,
      value_pred_loss_coef=0.5,
      gradient_clipping=0.5,
      debug_summaries=False,
      summarize_grads_and_vars=False)


# Define the replay buffer and metrics
replay_buffer_capacity = 1000
replay_buffer = tf_uniform_replay_buffer.TFUniformReplayBuffer(
      ppo.collect_data_spec,
      batch_size=env.batch_size,
      max_length=replay_buffer_capacity)
collect_metrics = [
      tf_metrics.AverageReturnMetric(
          buffer_size=replay_buffer_capacity),
      tf_metrics.EnvironmentSteps(),
      tf_metrics.NumberOfEpisodes(),
]


# Define the driver and training loop
initial_collect_steps = 1000
collect_steps_per_iteration = 1
num_iterations = 1000
collect_driver = DynamicStepDriver(
      env,
      ppo.collect_policy,
      observers=[replay_buffer.add_batch] + collect_metrics,
      num_steps=collect_steps_per_iteration)
initial_collect_driver = DynamicStepDriver(
      env,
      ppo.collect_policy,
      observers=[replay_buffer.add_batch] + ...
```

## 5.17 How can you implement advanced neural network architectures, such as dynamic computation graphs or neural architecture search, in TensorFlow?

TensorFlow is a versatile framework that allows researchers and practitioners to implement advanced neural network architectures. In this answer, we will discuss two such architectures: dynamic computation graphs and neural architecture search.

Dynamic Computation Graphs

TensorFlow's default mode of computation is static computation graphs. In this mode, the graph is defined upfront and cannot be changed at runtime. This can be limiting in some cases, such as when dealing with variable-length sequences or dynamic control flow.

To address this limitation, TensorFlow provides a dynamic computation graph mode through its eager execution API. In this mode, computations are executed eagerly, as they are defined, and the graph is not constructed upfront. This allows for more flexibility and enables the use of Python control flow statements such as loops and conditionals.

Here is an example of how to define a dynamic computation graph in TensorFlow:

python Copy code import tensorflow as tf

tf.enable_eager_execution()

# Define a function that computes the nth Fibonacci number recursively def fib(n): if n <= 1: return n else: return fib(n-1) + fib(n-2)

# Compute the 10th Fibonacci number result = fib(10)

# Print the result print(result)

In this example, we define a function that computes the nth Fibonacci number recursively using the dynamic computation graph mode in TensorFlow's eager execution API. We then compute the 10th Fibonacci number and print the result.

Neural Architecture Search

Neural architecture search (NAS) is a technique that automates the
process of neural network architecture design. NAS algorithms search
for the optimal architecture within a given search space, typically
using reinforcement learning or evolutionary algorithms.

TensorFlow provides a variety of tools and APIs for implementing
NAS. One popular approach is to use the Keras Tuner API, which
provides a high-level interface for hyperparameter tuning and model
architecture search.

Here is an example of how to use the Keras Tuner API to perform
NAS:

```python
import tensorflow as tf
from tensorflow import keras
from kerastuner.tuners import RandomSearch
from kerastuner.engine.hyperparameters import HyperParameters

# Define the search space
hp = HyperParameters()
hp.Choice('num_layers', [1, 2, 3])
hp.Choice('num_units', [32, 64, 128, 256])
hp.Choice('activation', ['relu', 'sigmoid', 'tanh'])

# Define the model
def build_model(hp):
    model = keras.Sequential()
    for i in range(hp.get('num_layers')):
        model.add(keras.layers.Dense(units=hp.get('num_units'),
            activation=hp.get('activation')))
        model.add(keras.layers.Dense(units=10, activation='softmax'))
        model.compile(optimizer='adam', loss='categorical_crossentropy
            ', metrics=['accuracy'])
    return model

# Define the tuner
tuner = RandomSearch(build_model, objective='val_accuracy',
    max_trials=10, hyperparameters=hp)

# Define the data
(x_train, y_train), (x_test, y_test) = keras.datasets.mnist.
    load_data()
x_train = x_train.reshape((60000, 28 * 28)).astype('float32') / 255
x_test = x_test.reshape((10000, 28 * 28)).astype('float32') / 255
y_train = keras.utils.to_categorical(y_train)
y_test = keras.utils.to_categorical(y_test)

# Perform the search
tuner.search(x_train, y_train, epochs=5, validation_data=(x_test,
    y_test))

# Get the best model and evaluate it on the test data
```

```
best_model = tuner.get_best_models(num_models=1)[0]
```

## 5.18  What are some advanced techniques for model compression in TensorFlow, such as knowledge distillation or weight sharing?

Model compression is an important technique to reduce the size and complexity of deep learning models without significantly sacrificing their performance. TensorFlow provides several methods for model compression, including knowledge distillation, weight pruning, and weight sharing. In this answer, we will discuss some advanced techniques for model compression in TensorFlow.

Knowledge distillation: Knowledge distillation is a technique that involves training a small student model to mimic the behavior of a larger teacher model. The student model learns from the outputs of the teacher model, which serves as a soft target. The goal is to transfer the knowledge of the larger model to the smaller model, while preserving its accuracy. TensorFlow provides an implementation of knowledge distillation in the tf.keras API. Here is an example:

```
# Define the teacher model
teacher_model = tf.keras.models.Sequential([
    tf.keras.layers.Conv2D(32, (3,3), activation='relu', input_shape
        =(28,28,1)),
    tf.keras.layers.MaxPooling2D(),
    tf.keras.layers.Flatten(),
    tf.keras.layers.Dense(128, activation='relu'),
    tf.keras.layers.Dense(10, activation='softmax')
])

# Define the student model
student_model = tf.keras.models.Sequential([
    tf.keras.layers.Conv2D(16, (3,3), activation='relu', input_shape
        =(28,28,1)),
    tf.keras.layers.MaxPooling2D(),
    tf.keras.layers.Flatten(),
    tf.keras.layers.Dense(64, activation='relu'),
    tf.keras.layers.Dense(10, activation='softmax')
])

# Define the loss function using the Kullback-Leibler divergence
def distillation_loss(y_true, y_pred):
    alpha = 0.1  # Temperature parameter
```

```
return (1 - alpha) * tf.keras.losses.categorical_crossentropy(
    y_true, y_pred) + alpha *    tf.keras.losses.
    kullback_leibler_divergence(y_true, y_pred)

# Train the student model using knowledge distillation
student_model.compile(loss=distillation_loss, optimizer='adam',
    metrics=['accuracy'])
history = student_model.fit(train_images, train_labels, epochs=10,
    validation_data=(test_images, test_labels), verbose=2)
```

Weight pruning: Weight pruning is a technique that involves removing the connections with small weight magnitudes from a neural network. This reduces the number of parameters and can lead to faster inference and reduced memory requirements. TensorFlow provides an implementation of weight pruning in the tfmot.sparsity.keras API. Here is an example:

```
import tensorflow_model_optimization as tfmot

# Define the model
model = tf.keras.models.Sequential([
    tf.keras.layers.Conv2D(32, (3,3), activation='relu', input_shape
        =(28,28,1)),
    tf.keras.layers.MaxPooling2D(),
    tf.keras.layers.Flatten(),
    tf.keras.layers.Dense(128, activation='relu'),
    tf.keras.layers.Dense(10, activation='softmax')
])

# Convert the model to a sparsity-enabled model
pruning_params = {'pruning_schedule': tfmot.sparsity.keras.
    PolynomialDecay(initial_sparsity=0.5, final_sparsity=0.9,
    begin_step=0, end_step=1000)}
pruned_model = tfmot.sparsity.keras.prune_low_magnitude(model, **
    pruning_params)

# Train the pruned model
pruned_model.compile(loss='categorical_crossentropy', optimizer='
    adam', metrics=['accuracy'])
pruned_model.fit(train_images, train_labels, epochs=10,
    validation_data=(test_images, test_labels), verbose=2)

# Convert the pruned model to a regular model
final_model = tfmot.sparsity.keras.strip_pruning(pruned_model)
```

## 5.19 How can you use TensorFlow for edge computing and implementing machine learning models on IoT devices?

TensorFlow is a versatile framework that can be used for various machine learning applications, including edge computing and implementing machine learning models on IoT devices. The main challenge of edge computing is the limited resources available on these devices, including processing power, memory, and energy. Therefore, it is crucial to optimize machine learning models to fit these constraints.

There are several techniques that can be used to optimize machine learning models for edge computing using TensorFlow. Some of these techniques include:

Quantization: Quantization is a technique that reduces the precision of the weights and activations in a model. This reduces the amount of memory required to store the model and improves its inference speed. TensorFlow supports both post-training and during-training quantization.

Pruning: Pruning is a technique that removes unnecessary connections between neurons in a neural network, reducing its size and computational complexity. TensorFlow provides various pruning techniques, including weight pruning, neuron pruning, and filter pruning.

Knowledge distillation: Knowledge distillation is a technique that transfers knowledge from a large, complex model to a smaller, simpler model. This technique can be used to create lightweight models that can run on edge devices without sacrificing performance.

Model compression: Model compression is a technique that reduces the size of a model by compressing its parameters, weights, or gradients. TensorFlow provides several compression techniques, including weight sharing, quantization, and pruning.

To implement machine learning models on IoT devices using TensorFlow, developers can use TensorFlow Lite, a version of TensorFlow optimized for mobile and embedded devices. TensorFlow Lite provides a lightweight runtime that can run machine learning models on resource-constrained devices. It also provides tools for model conversion and optimization, making it easy to deploy models to these devices.

In conclusion, TensorFlow provides a wide range of techniques and tools for optimizing machine learning models for edge computing and implementing them on IoT devices. These techniques can help reduce the memory, computation, and energy requirements of machine learning models, making them more suitable for edge computing applications.

## 5.20    How do you handle security and privacy concerns when training and deploying TensorFlow models, such as differential privacy or secure multiparty computation?

Security and privacy are critical concerns when it comes to machine learning, especially when working with sensitive data. TensorFlow provides several tools and techniques for ensuring the security and privacy of models during training and deployment.

One of the main techniques for privacy preservation in TensorFlow is differential privacy. Differential privacy is a technique for protecting the privacy of individuals in a dataset by adding random noise to the data before sharing it. This random noise makes it harder for an attacker to identify individual data points in the dataset, while still preserving the overall statistical properties of the data.

TensorFlow provides a library for implementing differential privacy, called TensorFlow Privacy. This library includes tools for adding differential privacy to various machine learning algorithms, such as deep neural networks, linear models, and decision trees. For example, to add differential privacy to a deep neural network, you can use the TensorFlow Privacy library to add noise to the gradients computed during training. This helps to protect the privacy of the training data while still allowing the model to learn useful patterns.

Another important technique for ensuring security in TensorFlow is secure multi-party computation (MPC). Secure MPC is a technique for computing the output of a machine learning model without revealing the input data to anyone. This is especially important in scenarios where multiple parties want to collaborate on a machine learning task without revealing their private data.

TensorFlow provides several tools for implementing secure MPC, such as TensorFlow Federated and TensorFlow Encrypted. TensorFlow Federated is a framework for building distributed machine learning models, where data is stored and processed on different devices without being shared. TensorFlow Encrypted is a library for implementing secure MPC using cryptographic techniques such as homomorphic encryption and secret sharing.

In addition to these techniques, TensorFlow provides several tools for ensuring model security during deployment. For example, TensorFlow Lite is a framework for deploying machine learning models on mobile and IoT devices. TensorFlow Lite includes features such as model quantization, which reduces the size of the model while preserving its accuracy, and model optimization, which improves the speed and efficiency of the model on resource-constrained devices.

Overall, TensorFlow provides several tools and techniques for ensuring the security and privacy of machine learning models during training and deployment. By using these tools and techniques, machine learning practitioners can build more secure and privacy-preserving models for a variety of applications.

# Chapter 6

# Guru

## 6.1 Can you discuss the design principles and trade-offs that influenced Tensor-Flow's architecture, and how they compare to other deep learning frameworks?

TensorFlow was designed with the goal of providing a scalable and flexible platform for building and deploying machine learning models. The architecture of TensorFlow was heavily influenced by a number of design principles, including modularity, extensibility, and performance.

One of the key features of TensorFlow is its use of a computational graph, which allows for efficient execution of complex models across multiple devices. The graph is constructed by defining a series of operations that can be executed in parallel, and TensorFlow automatically manages the data flow between them.

TensorFlow also includes a number of high-level APIs, such as Keras and Estimators, which provide a simple and intuitive way to build and train models. These APIs abstract away many of the lower-level details of TensorFlow, making it easier for developers to get started with machine learning.

In addition to its high-level APIs, TensorFlow also provides a number of low-level APIs for building custom operations and optimizing performance. For example, TensorFlow's XLA (Accelerated Linear Algebra) compiler can be used to automatically optimize the performance of computational graphs on a variety of hardware platforms.

One of the key trade-offs in TensorFlow's design is between ease-of-use and flexibility. While the high-level APIs make it easy to get started with machine learning, they can be limiting for more advanced use cases. On the other hand, the low-level APIs provide greater flexibility, but can be more difficult to work with.

Overall, TensorFlow's architecture has made it one of the most widely used and powerful deep learning frameworks available, with a large and active community of developers contributing to its ongoing development and improvement.

## 6.2   How do you optimize TensorFlow performance for large-scale, distributed training on heterogeneous hardware architectures, such as multi-GPU and multi-TPU systems?

Optimizing TensorFlow performance for large-scale, distributed training on heterogeneous hardware architectures involves a few key strategies, such as using distributed training APIs, optimizing data loading and preprocessing, and implementing model parallelism.

One of the most important tools for optimizing distributed training in TensorFlow is the tf.distribute module. This module provides a set of high-level APIs for distributing training across multiple devices, such as GPUs or TPUs, and across multiple machines. The module supports a range of distribution strategies, including synchronous and asynchronous training, parameter server training, and collective all-reduce training.

Another key strategy for optimizing TensorFlow performance in distributed training is optimizing data loading and preprocessing. This involves techniques such as sharding and caching data to reduce the amount of data that needs to be loaded into memory, using efficient data formats such as TFRecords or Apache Arrow, and using data augmentation to increase the diversity of the data.

To further optimize performance, model parallelism can be used to distribute the computation of a single model across multiple devices or machines. This can be done by splitting the model into multiple parts, each of which is executed on a separate device or machine, and passing data between the parts.

Additionally, other techniques such as mixed precision training, where the model weights are stored using a lower precision format to reduce memory requirements, and XLA (Accelerated Linear Algebra), which optimizes matrix operations in the model, can also be used to further improve performance.

Overall, optimizing TensorFlow performance for large-scale, distributed training on heterogeneous hardware architectures requires a combination of techniques and tools, and often involves a trade-off between performance and ease of use. However, with the right strategies and tools, it is possible to achieve high levels of performance and scalability in TensorFlow.

## 6.3   How can you implement advanced neural network techniques, such as neural Turing machines or memory-augmented neural networks, using TensorFlow?

Neural networks can be augmented with external memory systems to increase their memory capacity and allow them to perform tasks that require long-term memory, such as sequence-to-sequence tasks or navigation. Two popular memory-augmented neural network architectures are neural Turing machines (NTMs) and memory-augmented neural networks (MANNs).

In TensorFlow, these architectures can be implemented using the tf.raw_ops module, which allows for more flexibility in defining cus-

tom operations.  Here's an example of implementing a basic NTM
architecture in TensorFlow:

```python
import tensorflow as tf

class NTM(tf.keras.Model):
    def __init__(self, num_units, memory_size, memory_dim, output_dim
        ):
        super(NTM, self).__init__()

        # Initialize controller
        self.controller = tf.keras.layers.Dense(num_units)

        # Initialize memory
        self.memory = tf.Variable(tf.zeros((memory_size, memory_dim)))

        # Initialize read and write heads
        self.read_head = tf.Variable(tf.zeros(memory_dim))
        self.write_head = tf.Variable(tf.zeros(memory_dim))

        # Initialize output layer
        self.output_layer = tf.keras.layers.Dense(output_dim)

    def call(self, inputs):
        # Split inputs into input vector and control signal
        input_vector, control_signal = tf.split(inputs, [self.
            memory_dim, self.num_units])

        # Compute control signal with controller
        control_signal = self.controller(control_signal)

        # Compute read weights using content-based addressing
        content_similarity = tf.matmul(self.memory, input_vector,
            transpose_b=True)
        read_weights = tf.nn.softmax(content_similarity)

        # Read from memory using read weights
        read_vector = tf.reduce_sum(read_weights[:, tf.newaxis, :] *
            self.memory, axis=-1)

        # Compute write weights using content-based and location-based
            addressing
        content_similarity = tf.matmul(self.memory, input_vector,
            transpose_b=True)
        location_similarity = tf.matmul(self.memory, self.write_head,
            transpose_b=True)
        write_weights = tf.nn.softmax(content_similarity +
            location_similarity)

        # Write to memory using write weights and input vector
        self.memory.assign(tf.reduce_sum(write_weights[:, tf.newaxis,
            :] * input_vector[:, tf.newaxis, :], axis=0))

        # Update read and write heads
        self.read_head.assign(tf.reduce_sum(read_weights[:, tf.newaxis
            , :] * self.memory, axis=0))
        self.write_head.assign(tf.reduce_sum(write_weights[:, tf.
            newaxis, :] * input_vector[:, tf.newaxis, :], axis=0))

        # Concatenate read head and control signal and pass through
            output layer
        output = self.output_layer(tf.concat([self.read_head,
```

```
        control_signal], axis=-1))

    return output
```

In this example, we define an NTM model as a subclass of tf.keras.Model. The model consists of a controller, a memory bank, and read and write heads. The controller is a fully connected layer that takes the control signal as input and produces a control signal for the memory. The memory bank is represented as a tensor of size (memory_size, memory_dim), where memory_size is the number of memory slots and memory_dim is the dimensionality of each slot. The read and write heads are vectors of size memory_dim that are used to read from and write to the memory bank.

The call method of the model takes an input vector and a control signal as input. The input vector is used to read from and write to the memory bank, while the control signal is passed through the controller to produce a control signal for the memory. The input vector is split into two parts: one part is used for content-based addressing to compute the read and write weights, and the other part is used to

## 6.4    Can you discuss the challenges and opportunities of using TensorFlow for real-time machine learning applications, such as robotics or autonomous vehicles?

TensorFlow can be used for real-time machine learning applications such as robotics or autonomous vehicles. However, there are several challenges that need to be addressed, including:

Latency: Real-time applications require very low latency, which can be a challenge when running machine learning models that are computationally intensive. To reduce latency, it may be necessary to optimize the model architecture or use specialized hardware such as GPUs or TPUs.

Robustness: In real-time applications, the machine learning model needs to be robust to variations in input data and other environmental factors. This requires careful selection of training data, preprocessing techniques, and model architecture.

Data collection: Real-time applications may require large amounts of data to be collected in real-time, which can be challenging. This may require specialized hardware or software to capture and process the data.

Model deployment: Real-time applications require models to be deployed and updated quickly and reliably. This may require specialized deployment techniques such as containerization or edge computing.

Despite these challenges, there are also many opportunities for using TensorFlow in real-time applications. For example, TensorFlow's support for distributed training can be used to train models on large datasets quickly, while its support for GPUs and TPUs can be used to accelerate inference in real-time. Additionally, TensorFlow's flexibility and modularity make it well-suited for building custom models tailored to specific applications.

## 6.5   How do you perform model interpretability and explainability in TensorFlow, and what are the best practices for understanding and visualizing the inner workings of complex models?

Model interpretability and explainability are essential for understanding the inner workings of complex machine learning models and gaining insights into how they arrive at their predictions. In TensorFlow, there are several techniques for model interpretability and explainability, ranging from simple techniques like visualization to more advanced techniques like saliency maps and attention mechanisms.

Here are some of the key techniques for model interpretability and explainability in TensorFlow:

Visualization: One of the simplest and most effective ways to interpret a TensorFlow model is to visualize its output. This can be done using various tools and libraries, such as TensorBoard, which allows you to visualize the training process and output of your models.

Saliency Maps: Saliency maps are a technique for visualizing the input features that are most important for a given model's output. In TensorFlow, saliency maps can be generated using the GradientTape API, which allows you to compute gradients with respect to the input features.

Attention Mechanisms: Attention mechanisms are a technique for modeling the relationship between input features and output predictions. In TensorFlow, attention mechanisms can be implemented using the AttentionLayer class, which allows you to define custom attention mechanisms for your models.

Integrated Gradients: Integrated gradients is a technique for estimating the contribution of input features to a model's output. In TensorFlow, integrated gradients can be computed using the IntegratedGradients class, which is part of the tf-explain library.

LIME: Local Interpretable Model-Agnostic Explanations (LIME) is a technique for generating local explanations for a model's predictions. In TensorFlow, LIME can be implemented using the lime library, which allows you to generate explanations for any model that can produce a probability distribution over its output.

SHAP: SHapley Additive exPlanations (SHAP) is a technique for generating global explanations for a model's predictions. In TensorFlow, SHAP can be implemented using the shap library, which allows you to generate explanations for any model that can produce a probability distribution over its output.

In addition to these techniques, there are several best practices for model interpretability and explainability in TensorFlow, such as using simpler models that are easier to interpret, validating your models with real-world data, and involving domain experts in the interpretability process. By using these techniques and best practices, you can gain deeper insights into the inner workings of your TensorFlow models and ensure that they are making accurate and reliable predictions.

## 6.6    What are the key principles of continual learning, and how can you implement it using TensorFlow to achieve lifelong learning capabilities?

Continual learning, also known as lifelong learning or incremental learning, is a machine learning approach that involves learning from a stream of data over an extended period of time, without forgetting the previously learned knowledge. The goal is to create models that can learn continuously from new data, adapt to changes in the environment, and improve their performance over time.

TensorFlow provides several techniques for implementing continual learning, including:

Elastic weight consolidation (EWC): EWC is a regularization technique that assigns importance values to the parameters of the neural network based on their contribution to the model's performance on the previous tasks. When training on a new task, the importance values of the previous tasks are used to protect the parameters that are important for the old tasks, while allowing the other parameters to be updated. This approach can prevent catastrophic forgetting and maintain the performance of the previous tasks.

Learning without forgetting (LwF): LwF is a knowledge distillation technique that involves transferring the knowledge from the previous tasks to the new task by training the new model to predict the outputs of the old model on the previous tasks. This approach allows the new model to retain the knowledge of the previous tasks while learning the new task, preventing forgetting.

Progressive neural networks (PNN): PNN is an architecture design that involves creating a new neural network for each new task, but connecting the output of the previous network to the input of the new network. This approach allows the new network to leverage the features learned by the previous networks, while avoiding interference between the old and new tasks.

Here is an example of how to implement EWC in TensorFlow:

```
import tensorflow as tf
```

```
from tensorflow.keras import layers
from tensorflow_addons import optimizers

# Define the EWC loss function
def ewc_loss(model, old_params, importance):
    ewc_loss = 0
    for i, layer in enumerate(model.layers):
        if hasattr(layer, 'kernel'):
            ewc_loss += tf.reduce_sum(importance[i] * tf.square(layer.
                kernel - old_params[i]))
    return ewc_loss

# Define the model
model = tf.keras.Sequential([
    layers.Dense(64, activation='relu', input_shape=(784,)),
    layers.Dense(10, activation='softmax')
])

# Compile the model with EWC loss and Adam optimizer
old_params = model.get_weights()
importance = [tf.ones_like(w) for w in old_params]
model.compile(loss='categorical_crossentropy', optimizer=optimizers.
    Adam(),
    metrics=['accuracy', ewc_loss(model, old_params, importance)])

# Train the model on the first task
model.fit(x_train_task1, y_train_task1, epochs=10)

# Freeze the first task and compute the importance values
old_params = model.get_weights()
for layer in model.layers[:-1]:
    layer.trainable = False
importance = tf.gradients(model.output, model.layers[-2].output)[0]
    ** 2
importance /= tf.reduce_sum(importance)
importance = [tf.reshape(w, (-1,)) for w in importance]

# Train the model on the second task with EWC regularization
model.compile(loss='categorical_crossentropy', optimizer=optimizers.
    Adam(),
    metrics=['accuracy', ewc_loss(model, old_params, importance)])
model.fit(x_train_task2, y_train_task2, epochs=10)
```

In this example, we define the EWC loss function that computes the
regularization term based on the importance values of the parameters.
We then define a simple two-layer neural network and compile it with
EWC loss and Adam optimizer. We train the model on the first task
and freeze the first layer to compute the importance values for the
second task. Finally, we compile the model again with EWC

## 6.7    How can you use TensorFlow for multi-agent reinforcement learning, and what are the challenges and opportunities in this domain?

Multi-agent reinforcement learning is a subfield of reinforcement learning where multiple agents interact with each other and with the environment to learn to achieve a common goal. TensorFlow can be used to implement multi-agent reinforcement learning algorithms by defining the agents, the environment, and the communication between them.

One approach to implementing multi-agent reinforcement learning in TensorFlow is to use a centralized training and decentralized execution (CTDE) architecture. In this architecture, the agents share a centralized critic network that estimates the value function for each agent's action based on the joint state and action of all agents. Each agent has its own actor network that selects actions based on its local observation. During training, the critic network is updated using the joint observations and actions of all agents, while each agent's actor network is updated using only its local observation and action.

Another approach is to use a decentralized training and execution (DTE) architecture, where each agent has its own critic and actor networks, and the agents learn to coordinate with each other through local communication. This approach is more challenging because it requires the agents to learn to coordinate without a centralized signal, but it can lead to more scalable and robust solutions.

To implement multi-agent reinforcement learning in TensorFlow, one can use the TensorFlow Agents library, which provides a set of high-level APIs for building and training multi-agent systems. The library includes implementations of several state-of-the-art algorithms, such as MADDPG, COMA, and QMIX, as well as tools for visualizing and analyzing the training process.

Challenges in multi-agent reinforcement learning include the curse of dimensionality, where the state and action spaces grow exponentially with the number of agents, and the difficulty of learning to coordinate with other agents in a dynamic and complex environment. However, multi-agent reinforcement learning also offers opportunities for solving real-world problems that require cooperation and coordination between multiple agents, such as traffic control, robotic swarms, and online auctions.

## 6.8   Can you discuss the impact of hardware trends, such as neuromorphic computing or quantum computing, on TensorFlow's future development and capabilities?

Hardware trends, such as neuromorphic computing and quantum computing, are expected to have a significant impact on the future development and capabilities of TensorFlow.

Neuromorphic computing is a type of computing that is inspired by the human brain and nervous system. It uses parallel processing and low-power consumption to perform machine learning tasks more efficiently than traditional computing systems. TensorFlow has already started to incorporate neuromorphic computing concepts through the use of spiking neural networks, which are designed to simulate the behavior of neurons in the brain. These networks are particularly well-suited for tasks such as image recognition and audio processing.

Quantum computing, on the other hand, is an emerging technology that uses quantum mechanics to perform computations. It is still in its early stages, but it has the potential to revolutionize machine learning by allowing for much faster processing of large amounts of data. TensorFlow has already started to explore the potential of quantum computing through the development of TensorFlow Quantum, which is a framework for building and training quantum machine learning models.

In addition to these hardware trends, TensorFlow is also likely to be impacted by developments in other areas such as natural language processing, computer vision, and reinforcement learning. As these fields continue to evolve, TensorFlow will need to adapt and incorporate new techniques and algorithms to stay at the forefront of machine learning research and development.

Overall, the future of TensorFlow is closely tied to the development of
new hardware technologies and their applications to machine learning.
As these technologies continue to evolve and mature, it is likely that
TensorFlow will continue to push the boundaries of what is possible
in the field of machine learning.

## 6.9   How do you use TensorFlow to implement state-of-the-art models in natural language processing, such as BERT or GPT, and what are the best practices for fine-tuning and deploying these models?

TensorFlow is a popular open-source framework that is widely used in
natural language processing (NLP) for building state-of-the-art models. Some of the most well-known models in NLP, such as BERT and
GPT, have been implemented using TensorFlow. In this answer, we
will discuss the key principles of these models and how to implement
them using TensorFlow, as well as the best practices for fine-tuning
and deploying them.

BERT (Bidirectional Encoder Representations from Transformers) is
a powerful language model that was introduced in 2018. It is based
on the Transformer architecture and is pre-trained on a large corpus
of text data using a masked language modeling objective. The key
idea behind BERT is to use a bidirectional approach to capture the
context of a word, which allows it to better understand the meaning
of the words in a sentence.

To implement BERT using TensorFlow, there are several pre-trained
models that can be fine-tuned for specific NLP tasks, such as classification, question-answering, or named entity recognition. These
models are available through the TensorFlow Hub, and can be easily
imported and fine-tuned using TensorFlow's Keras API. Here is an
example of fine-tuning BERT for sentiment analysis on the IMDB

dataset:

```
import tensorflow as tf
import tensorflow_hub as hub
from tensorflow.keras.layers import Dense, Input
from tensorflow.keras.models import Model

# Load the pre-trained BERT model from TensorFlow Hub
bert_layer = hub.KerasLayer("https://tfhub.dev/tensorflow/
    bert_en_uncased_L-12_H-768_A-12/4", trainable=True)

# Define the input and output layers for the model
input_word_ids = Input(shape=(max_seq_length,), dtype=tf.int32, name
    ="input_word_ids")
input_mask = Input(shape=(max_seq_length,), dtype=tf.int32, name="
    input_mask")
segment_ids = Input(shape=(max_seq_length,), dtype=tf.int32, name="
    segment_ids")

# Apply the BERT layer to the input layers
pooled_output, sequence_output = bert_layer([input_word_ids,
    input_mask, segment_ids])

# Add a dense layer and output layer for classification
x = Dense(256, activation='relu')(pooled_output)
output = Dense(1, activation='sigmoid')(x)

# Define the model
model = Model(inputs=[input_word_ids, input_mask, segment_ids],
    outputs=output)

# Compile the model with an appropriate loss function and optimizer
model.compile(loss='binary_crossentropy', optimizer='adam', metrics
    =['accuracy'])

# Train the model on the IMDB dataset
model.fit(train_data, epochs=10, validation_data=val_data)
```

GPT (Generative Pre-trained Transformer) is another popular language model that is based on the Transformer architecture. It was introduced in 2019 and is pre-trained on a large corpus of text data using a language modeling objective. The key idea behind GPT is to use an autoregressive approach to generate text, which allows it to produce high-quality text samples that are similar to human writing.

To implement GPT using TensorFlow, there are several pre-trained models that can be used for text generation tasks, such as language modeling or text completion. These models are available through the Hugging Face Transformers library, which provides an easy-to-use interface for working with pre-trained language models.

# 6.10 What are the key principles of unsupervised or semi-supervised learning in TensorFlow, and how can you implement advanced techniques such as variational autoencoders or generative adversarial networks?

Unsupervised learning is a machine learning paradigm in which the model is trained on unlabeled data to discover patterns, relationships, and structure within the data without any explicit target labels. Semi-supervised learning, on the other hand, is a variant of supervised learning that involves training a model on a small amount of labeled data and a large amount of unlabeled data. In this case, the model uses the structure and patterns learned from the unlabeled data to improve its predictions on the labeled data.

TensorFlow provides several tools and APIs for implementing unsupervised and semi-supervised learning techniques, including variational autoencoders (VAEs) and generative adversarial networks (GANs). These models are commonly used for tasks such as image generation, data compression, and anomaly detection.

Variational autoencoders (VAEs) are a type of generative model that learn to map the input data to a latent space representation and then reconstruct the original data from the latent space representation. VAEs are trained using a loss function that measures the difference between the input data and the reconstructed data, as well as the divergence between the distribution of the latent space and a prior distribution. The loss function is optimized using stochastic gradient descent or other optimization algorithms.

Here's an example of implementing a VAE using TensorFlow:

```
import tensorflow as tf

# Define the encoder model
encoder = tf.keras.Sequential([
    tf.keras.layers.Input(shape=(28, 28, 1)),
    tf.keras.layers.Conv2D(filters=32, kernel_size=3, strides=(2, 2),
        activation='relu'),
    tf.keras.layers.Conv2D(filters=64, kernel_size=3, strides=(2, 2),
        activation='relu'),
    tf.keras.layers.Flatten(),
```

```
      tf.keras.layers.Dense(units=256, activation='relu'),
      tf.keras.layers.Dense(units=128, activation='relu'),
      tf.keras.layers.Dense(units=32, activation='relu')
])

# Define the decoder model
decoder = tf.keras.Sequential([
   tf.keras.layers.Input(shape=(32,)),
   tf.keras.layers.Dense(units=128, activation='relu'),
   tf.keras.layers.Dense(units=256, activation='relu'),
   tf.keras.layers.Reshape(target_shape=(4, 4, 16)),
   tf.keras.layers.Conv2DTranspose(filters=64, kernel_size=3,
      strides=(2, 2), padding='same', activation='relu'),
   tf.keras.layers.Conv2DTranspose(filters=32, kernel_size=3,
      strides=(2, 2), padding='same', activation='relu'),
   tf.keras.layers.Conv2DTranspose(filters=1, kernel_size=3, strides
      =(1, 1), padding='same', activation=None)
])


# Define the VAE model
class VAE(tf.keras.Model):
   def __init__(self, encoder, decoder, **kwargs):
      super(VAE, self).__init__(**kwargs)
      self.encoder = encoder
      self.decoder = decoder

   def call(self, inputs):
      # Encode the input data to a latent space representation
      z_mean, z_log_var, z = self.encode(inputs)
      # Reconstruct the input data from the latent space
         representation
      reconstructed = self.decode(z)
      # Return both the reconstructed data and the latent space
         representation
      return reconstructed, z_mean, z_log_var, z

   def encode(self, inputs):
      # Compute the mean and log variance of the latent space
         distribution
      x = self.encoder(inputs)
      z_mean = tf.keras.layers.Dense(units=32)(x)
      z_log_var = tf.keras.layers.Dense(units=32)(x)
      # Sample a point from the latent space distribution using the
         reparameterization trick
```

## 6.11   Can you discuss the challenges and opportunities of using TensorFlow for large-scale reinforcement learning applications, such as AlphaGo or OpenAI's Dactyl?

Reinforcement learning (RL) is a machine learning technique that enables an agent to learn optimal decision-making policies in a dynamic environment through trial-and-error interactions with the environment. TensorFlow is a popular deep learning library that provides powerful tools for building and training complex RL models.

Large-scale RL applications present unique challenges in terms of scalability, performance, and robustness. The sheer complexity and dimensionality of the state and action spaces in such applications often require sophisticated function approximation techniques, such as deep neural networks, to accurately model the underlying dynamics of the environment.

One of the key challenges in large-scale RL is the high computational cost of training deep RL models on large datasets. This requires specialized hardware, such as GPUs or TPUs, as well as efficient parallelization and distributed computing techniques, such as data parallelism or model parallelism.

Another challenge is the need for stable and robust optimization methods that can handle the inherent non-stationarity and high variance of the RL problem. Techniques such as proximal policy optimization (PPO) and deep Q-networks (DQN) have been developed to address these issues and have achieved state-of-the-art performance in a variety of RL applications.

In addition to these technical challenges, large-scale RL applications also require careful consideration of ethical and safety implications, as well as the potential impact on society at large. Ensuring that RL models are aligned with human values and goals, and avoiding unintended consequences or negative externalities, is an important area of ongoing research.

Despite these challenges, large-scale RL applications hold tremendous promise in domains such as robotics, gaming, and finance, where intelligent agents can learn to make optimal decisions in complex and dynamic environments. TensorFlow's flexible and powerful APIs, combined with its scalability and performance optimizations, make it a natural choice for implementing large-scale RL systems.

## 6.12 How can you implement advanced optimization techniques in TensorFlow, such as stochastic weight averaging or lookahead optimizers, and what are their advantages and trade-offs?

In machine learning, optimization refers to the process of finding the best model parameters that minimize the loss function. TensorFlow provides a wide range of optimization techniques that can be used to train deep learning models. In addition to the standard optimization techniques, TensorFlow also supports several advanced optimization methods that can help improve the training efficiency and model performance. In this answer, we will discuss two such techniques: stochastic weight averaging and lookahead optimizers.

Stochastic Weight Averaging: Stochastic Weight Averaging (SWA) is a simple and effective optimization technique that can be used to improve the generalization performance of deep learning models. The basic idea behind SWA is to take the running average of the weights during training instead of the final weight values. This can help the model to escape from local minima and improve its generalization performance.

In TensorFlow, SWA can be implemented by modifying the training loop to perform a running average of the weights during the training process. For example, the following code snippet shows how to implement SWA for a convolutional neural network (CNN) in TensorFlow:

```
optimizer = tf.keras.optimizers.SGD(lr=0.01)
model.compile(loss='categorical_crossentropy', optimizer=optimizer,
    metrics=['accuracy'])

swa = tf.keras.callbacks.LambdaCallback(on_epoch_end=lambda epoch,
    logs: update_weights(model, epoch))
```

```
model.fit(x_train, y_train, epochs=10, batch_size=32, callbacks=[swa
    ])
```

Here, we define a custom callback function called update_weights that updates the weights of the model with their running average at the end of each epoch. This callback function can be defined as follows:

```
def update_weights(model, epoch):
    if epoch >= 5:
        weight_average = tf.keras.models.clone_model(model)
        weight_average.set_weights(model.get_weights())
        model_weights = model.get_weights()
        weight_average_weights = weight_average.get_weights()
        for i, weights in enumerate(model_weights):
            weight_average_weights[i] = np.mean([weights,
                weight_average_weights[i]], axis=0)
        weight_average.set_weights(weight_average_weights)
        model.set_weights(weight_average.get_weights())
```

Lookahead Optimizers: Lookahead optimization is another advanced optimization technique that can be used to improve the training efficiency and performance of deep learning models. The basic idea behind lookahead optimization is to use a second optimizer to look ahead and update the weights before the main optimizer updates them. This can help the model to converge faster and reach a better optimum.

In TensorFlow, lookahead optimization can be implemented using the Lookahead optimizer, which takes two optimizer objects as input: a main optimizer and a lookahead optimizer. The lookahead optimizer is used to update the weights ahead of the main optimizer, and the main optimizer is used to update the weights normally. The following code snippet shows how to implement lookahead optimization for a CNN in TensorFlow:

```
optimizer = tf.keras.optimizers.SGD(lr=0.01)
lookahead = tfa.optimizers.Lookahead(optimizer, sync_period=5,
    slow_step_size=0.5)
model.compile(loss='categorical_crossentropy', optimizer=lookahead,
    metrics=['accuracy'])

model.fit(x_train, y_train, epochs=10, batch_size=32)
```

Here, we define the Lookahead optimizer by passing the main optimizer object (optimizer) as input, along with the sync_period and slow_step_size parameters. The sync_period parameter specifies how often the lookahead optimizer should update the weights, and

the slow_step_size parameter specifies how much weight the lookahead optimizer should put on the current update. In this example,
the lookahead optimizer updates the weights every 5 steps and uses
a slow step size of 0.5.

## 6.13 What are the key principles of neu-roevolution, and how can you imple-ment it using TensorFlow to evolve neural network architectures and hy-perparameters?

Neuroevolution is an approach to train neural networks by using evolutionary algorithms, such as genetic algorithms or evolution strategies. The key idea is to treat the neural network's architecture and
hyperparameters as a set of parameters that can be optimized through
a process of evolution. In other words, instead of manually designing
the neural network's architecture and hyperparameters, neuroevolution allows the model to evolve through a process of natural selection.

The general process of neuroevolution involves the following steps:

Initialization: The population of neural networks is randomly generated with a set of initial weights, architecture, and hyperparameters.
Evaluation: The fitness function is defined, which evaluates the performance of each neural network in the population. Selection: The
fittest neural networks are selected to reproduce, based on their fitness scores. This can be done using techniques such as tournament
selection or roulette wheel selection. Crossover and Mutation: The
selected neural networks are used to generate offspring through the
process of crossover and mutation. Crossover involves combining the
weights, architecture, and hyperparameters of two neural networks
to create a new one, while mutation involves randomly changing the
weights, architecture, or hyperparameters of a neural network. Re-
placement: The new offspring replaces some of the old neural networks in the population. Repeat: Steps 2-5 are repeated until the
population converges, or a desired level of performance is achieved.

To implement neuroevolution in TensorFlow, we can use the Tensor-

Flow Evolution Strategy (ES) API. This API provides a set of tools and functions for implementing evolution strategies, which is a type of neuroevolution that is particularly well-suited for training large-scale neural networks. Here's an example code snippet that uses the TensorFlow ES API to train a neural network on the MNIST dataset:

```python
import tensorflow as tf
from tensorflow.keras.datasets import mnist

# Load the MNIST dataset
(x_train, y_train), (x_test, y_test) = mnist.load_data()

# Normalize the data
x_train = x_train / 255.0
x_test = x_test / 255.0

# Define the fitness function
def fitness_fn(model):
    model.compile(loss='sparse_categorical_crossentropy', optimizer='
        adam', metrics=['accuracy'])
    model.fit(x_train, y_train, epochs=1, batch_size=32,
        validation_data=(x_test, y_test))
    return model.evaluate(x_test, y_test, verbose=0)[1]

# Define the ES optimizer
optimizer = tf.keras.optimizers.Adam()

# Define the ES strategy
strategy = tf.distribute.MirroredStrategy()
    es = tf.keras.estimator.experimental.EsStrategy(
        population_size=10, sigma=0.1, learning_rate=0.1, optimizer=
            optimizer, strategy=strategy)

# Define the model
def create_model():
model = tf.keras.Sequential([
    tf.keras.layers.Flatten(input_shape=(28, 28)),
    tf.keras.layers.Dense(128, activation='relu'),
    tf.keras.layers.Dense(10, activation='softmax')
])
return model

# Train the model using ES
estimator = tf.keras.estimator.model_to_estimator(
keras_model=create_model(), model_dir='./checkpoints', config=tf.
    estimator.RunConfig())
    estimator.train(fitness_fn, steps=100, max_iterations=10,
        early_stopping_rounds=2, population_strategy=es)
```

In this example, we define the fitness function as the accuracy of the model on the test set after training it for one epoch on the training set. We then define the ES optimizer and strategy, and create a simple neural network model.

## 6.14 How can you use TensorFlow to implement state-of-the-art models in computer vision, such as EfficientNet or ResNeXt, and what are the best practices for training and deploying these models?

TensorFlow is a popular open-source deep learning framework that can be used to build and train state-of-the-art models in computer vision. Some of the most widely used models in this field are EfficientNet and ResNeXt.

EfficientNet is a family of convolutional neural networks (CNNs) that achieve state-of-the-art performance on various computer vision tasks, while requiring fewer parameters and less computation compared to other models. The key principle behind EfficientNet is to use a compound scaling method that balances the model's depth, width, and resolution at each stage of the network, thereby optimizing the trade-off between accuracy and efficiency.

To implement EfficientNet using TensorFlow, one can use the pre-trained models provided by the TensorFlow Hub. TensorFlow Hub is a repository of pre-trained models and modules that can be easily integrated into TensorFlow projects. For example, to use the pre-trained EfficientNetB0 model in a TensorFlow project, one can load the model using the following code:

```
import tensorflow_hub as hub
import tensorflow as tf

module_url = "https://tfhub.dev/google/efficientnet/b0/feature-
    vector/1"
model = tf.keras.Sequential([
    hub.KerasLayer(module_url, trainable=False),
    tf.keras.layers.Dense(num_classes, activation='softmax')
])
```

Here, we load the pre-trained EfficientNetB0 feature extractor from TensorFlow Hub and add a dense layer on top of it to perform classification. The trainable=False argument ensures that the pre-trained weights are frozen and not updated during training, thereby preserving the learned representations.

ResNeXt, on the other hand, is a family of deep residual networks that achieves state-of-the-art accuracy on various computer vision tasks. The key principle behind ResNeXt is to use a modular block design that leverages grouped convolutions to capture multiple views of the same feature maps, thereby improving the model's representational power.

To implement ResNeXt using TensorFlow, one can use the pre-trained models provided by the TensorFlow Model Garden. The TensorFlow Model Garden is a repository of state-of-the-art models and training scripts that can be easily adapted to different computer vision tasks. For example, to fine-tune the pre-trained ResNet50 model on a custom image classification task using transfer learning, one can use the following code:

```
import tensorflow as tf
import tensorflow_hub as hub

# Load the pre-trained ResNet50 model from TensorFlow Hub
module_url = "https://tfhub.dev/google/imagenet/resnet_v2_50/
    feature_vector/4"
feature_extractor = hub.KerasLayer(module_url, input_shape=(224,
    224, 3), trainable=False)

# Build a classification model on top of the feature extractor
model = tf.keras.Sequential([
    feature_extractor,
    tf.keras.layers.Dense(1024, activation='relu'),
    tf.keras.layers.Dropout(0.5),
    tf.keras.layers.Dense(num_classes, activation='softmax')
])

# Compile the model and prepare the data
model.compile(optimizer='adam', loss='categorical_crossentropy',
    metrics=['accuracy'])
train_data, val_data = get_data_generators()

# Fine-tune the model on the custom data
model.fit(train_data, epochs=10, validation_data=val_data)
```

Here, we load the pre-trained ResNet50 feature extractor from TensorFlow Hub and build a classification model on top of it using transfer learning. The trainable=False argument ensures that the pre-trained weights are frozen and not updated during training. We then compile the model using the Adam optimizer and categorical cross-entropy loss, and prepare the data using data generators. Finally, we fine-tune the model on the custom data for 10 epochs using the fit method.

# 6.15 How do you use TensorFlow to address fairness, accountability, and transparency in machine learning, and what are the best practices for mitigating biases in model training and deployment?

Fairness, accountability, and transparency (FAT) are increasingly important considerations in machine learning, particularly when the models are used in sensitive areas such as finance, healthcare, and criminal justice. TensorFlow provides several tools and techniques to address these concerns.

One of the key challenges in FAT is addressing biases in the data and the model. TensorFlow provides tools for exploring and visualizing data, which can help identify biases in the dataset. For example, the Facets Overview and Facets Dive tools can be used to visualize large datasets and identify potential biases in the data. The TensorFlow Data Validation (TFDV) library can be used to validate data for consistency and accuracy, and to detect and fix data skew or imbalance.

Another approach to addressing biases is to use algorithms that are inherently fair, such as those based on counterfactual fairness or individual fairness. TensorFlow provides several libraries and frameworks that support these approaches, such as the AI Fairness 360 toolkit and the FairLearn library.

Another important aspect of FAT is ensuring accountability and transparency in the model. TensorFlow provides tools for monitoring and explaining the behavior of the model, such as the TensorFlow Model Analysis (TFMA) library and the TensorFlow Explainability (TFX) library. These tools can help identify the features and inputs that are most important to the model's decision-making process, and can provide insights into the model's behavior and performance.

Finally, it is important to ensure that the model is transparent and understandable to end-users and stakeholders. TensorFlow provides several tools for generating human-readable summaries and visualizations of the model, such as the TensorFlow Lite Model Viewer and

the What-If Tool. These tools can help stakeholders understand how
the model works and make informed decisions about its use.

In summary, TensorFlow provides a variety of tools and techniques to
address fairness, accountability, and transparency in machine learning. By using these tools and following best practices, developers can
ensure that their models are both effective and ethical.

## 6.16 Can you discuss the challenges and opportunities of using TensorFlow for multi-modal and multi-task learning in complex, real-world applications?

Multi-modal learning is a subfield of machine learning that deals with
models capable of processing and learning from multiple input modalities, such as images, text, and audio. Multi-task learning is another
subfield that deals with models capable of performing multiple tasks
simultaneously, sharing common representations between them to improve performance.  Both techniques are widely used in complex,
real-world applications, such as autonomous vehicles, robotics, and
natural language processing.

TensorFlow provides a set of APIs and tools that enable developers
to implement multi-modal and multi-task learning models efficiently.
Some of the key features and techniques that can be used in Tensor-
Flow include:

Multiple input modalities: TensorFlow provides various data processing and loading APIs, such as tf.data and tf.io, that can handle
various input modalities, such as images, text, and audio, efficiently.
These APIs can also be used to preprocess and augment data, such
as data normalization and data augmentation, to improve model performance.

Multi-modal fusion: In multi-modal learning, the challenge is to combine the information from different input modalities effectively. TensorFlow provides various fusion techniques, such as early fusion, late
fusion, and cross-modal attention, that can be used to combine infor-

mation from different modalities.

Multi-task learning: TensorFlow also provides APIs for building multi-task learning models, such as the Keras functional API, that allows developers to build complex models with shared layers and shared weights. This enables the model to learn multiple tasks simultaneously, sharing common representations between them, which can improve the overall model performance.

Transfer learning: Transfer learning is another technique widely used in multi-modal and multi-task learning, where a model pre-trained on a large dataset is fine-tuned for a specific task or modality. TensorFlow provides various pre-trained models, such as ImageNet and BERT, that can be fine-tuned for specific tasks or modalities efficiently.

Custom layers and models: TensorFlow also allows developers to implement custom layers and models, which can be used to implement novel multi-modal and multi-task learning techniques. This enables developers to experiment with various architectures and techniques, tailoring them to specific use cases and applications.

Overall, TensorFlow provides a rich set of APIs and tools that enable developers to implement multi-modal and multi-task learning models efficiently. By leveraging these features and techniques, developers can build complex, real-world applications that process and learn from multiple input modalities, improving model performance and accuracy.

## 6.17   How can you leverage TensorFlow to implement state-of-the-art models in speech recognition, such as Wav2Vec or DeepSpeech, and what are the best practices for training and deploying these models?

TensorFlow is a popular deep learning framework that can be used to implement state-of-the-art models in various domains, including speech recognition. In this context, the goal is to transcribe speech signals into text, a task that has been addressed using a variety of deep learning architectures.

One of the key principles of state-of-the-art speech recognition models is the use of deep neural networks, such as convolutional neural networks (CNNs) or recurrent neural networks (RNNs), to process the raw audio signals and extract relevant features. These features are then fed into another neural network, such as a fully connected neural network or a transformer-based model, to perform the actual transcription.

Here are some examples of state-of-the-art speech recognition models that can be implemented using TensorFlow:

Wav2Vec: This model, developed by Facebook AI Research, uses a CNN-based architecture to learn representations of raw audio signals without any pre-processing or feature extraction. These representations are then used as input to a transformer-based model for transcription.

To implement Wav2Vec in TensorFlow, one can use the TensorFlow Addons library, which provides a pre-trained Wav2Vec model that can be fine-tuned on a specific dataset. The library also includes tools for data preparation and feature extraction.

DeepSpeech: This model, developed by Mozilla, uses a RNN-based architecture to transcribe speech signals. It is trained end-to-end, meaning that it takes raw audio signals as input and produces text output without any intermediate pre-processing or feature extraction.

To implement DeepSpeech in TensorFlow, one can use the TensorFlow Speech Recognition library, which provides pre-trained models and tools for data preparation and feature extraction. The library also includes support for transfer learning, which can be used to fine-tune a pre-trained model on a specific dataset.

In addition to these models, TensorFlow also provides tools for speech synthesis, such as the Tacotron 2 and WaveGlow models, which can be used to generate speech signals from text input.

When training and deploying speech recognition models in Tensor-Flow, it is important to consider the following best practices:

Data augmentation: Speech recognition models can benefit from data augmentation techniques, such as adding noise or changing the pitch of the input signals. This can help the model generalize better to new, unseen data.

Transfer learning: Pre-trained models can be fine-tuned on specific datasets, which can save time and resources compared to training a model from scratch.

Model optimization: Speech recognition models can be computationally intensive, so it is important to optimize the model architecture and hyperparameters for maximum performance. This can include techniques such as pruning, quantization, and mixed-precision training.

Bias mitigation: Speech recognition models can be prone to biases, such as gender or dialect biases. It is important to evaluate and mitigate these biases in the model training and deployment process to ensure fair and accurate results for all users.

## 6.18    What are the key principles of adversarial robustness, and how can you implement it using TensorFlow to defend against adversarial attacks on machine learning models?

Adversarial robustness is the ability of a machine learning model to withstand intentional or unintentional attempts to subvert its performance. Adversarial attacks can be classified as either white-box or black-box, depending on whether the attacker has access to the model's parameters and architecture or not. In recent years, researchers have proposed several techniques to improve the adversarial robustness of machine learning models, such as adversarial training, randomized smoothing, and certified defense.

TensorFlow provides several tools and libraries to implement adversarial robustness techniques in machine learning models. Some of the key components of TensorFlow that can be used for adversarial robustness are:

Adversarial example generation: TensorFlow provides libraries such as CleverHans and ART (Adversarial Robustness Toolbox) that can be used to generate adversarial examples for a given machine learning model. These libraries implement various attack methods such as Fast Gradient Sign Method (FGSM), Projected Gradient Descent (PGD), and Carlini-Wagner (CW) attack.

Adversarial training: Adversarial training is a technique that involves training a machine learning model with both clean and adversarial examples to improve its adversarial robustness. TensorFlow provides a convenient way to perform adversarial training using the tf.Gradient-Tape API, which allows gradients to be computed with respect to arbitrary tensors.

Randomized smoothing: Randomized smoothing is a technique that involves adding random noise to inputs to improve the robustness of machine learning models. TensorFlow provides support for randomized smoothing via the tfp.distributions.Normal class, which can be used to add Gaussian noise to inputs.

Certified defense: Certified defense is a technique that involves proving the robustness of a machine learning model mathematically. TensorFlow provides libraries such as the Robustness Certification Toolbox (RCT) and Fast-Lin that can be used to implement certified defense.

Model compression: Model compression techniques such as knowledge distillation and pruning can be used to improve the adversarial robustness of machine learning models by reducing their complexity and making them less vulnerable to adversarial attacks.

Overall, TensorFlow provides a wide range of tools and libraries that can be used to implement adversarial robustness in machine learning models. However, it is important to note that achieving high levels of adversarial robustness remains a challenging research problem, and there is still much work to be done in this area.

## 6.19 How can you use TensorFlow to implement state-of-the-art models in generative modeling, such as StyleGAN or BigGAN, and what are the best practices for training and deploying these models?

Generative modeling is a subfield of machine learning that focuses on creating models that can generate data that is similar to a given dataset. Some of the popular generative models include Variational Autoencoders (VAEs), Generative Adversarial Networks (GANs), and Autoregressive models. TensorFlow is a popular framework for implementing these models, and it provides a variety of tools and APIs to facilitate the process.

Here are some of the steps involved in implementing state-of-the-art generative models in TensorFlow:

Data preparation: The first step is to prepare the training data. This involves collecting a large dataset of images, videos, or other types of data that you want the generative model to learn from. The data should be preprocessed and normalized to ensure that it is suitable for training the model.

Model selection: The next step is to choose the type of generative model that you want to use. This will depend on the specific task you are trying to solve and the properties of the dataset. For example, GANs are often used for generating images, while VAEs are used for image reconstruction and data compression.

Model architecture: Once you have selected the type of model, the next step is to design the model architecture. This involves choosing the number and types of layers, the activation functions, and the optimization algorithms. In TensorFlow, you can use the Keras API to design and build the model architecture.

Training: The next step is to train the generative model using the prepared dataset. This involves selecting the appropriate loss function, setting the learning rate, and choosing the batch size. You can use the fit() method in Keras to train the model.

Validation: Once the model is trained, the next step is to validate it using a separate dataset. This can help to ensure that the model is generalizing well to new data and is not overfitting to the training data.

Deployment: Finally, once the model is trained and validated, it can be deployed to generate new data. This can involve using the model to generate images, videos, or other types of data that are similar to the training dataset.

In addition to the above steps, there are also several best practices for implementing generative models in TensorFlow. These include using transfer learning to fine-tune pre-trained models, using data augmentation to increase the size of the training dataset, and using regularization techniques to prevent overfitting.

Overall, TensorFlow provides a powerful set of tools and APIs for implementing state-of-the-art generative models, and it is widely used in research and industry for a variety of applications.

## 6.20 Can you discuss the future directions of TensorFlow development and how it aligns with emerging trends in artificial intelligence, such as unsupervised learning, reinforcement learning, or transfer learning?

Certainly! TensorFlow has been rapidly evolving since its release, and it continues to be a leading framework in the field of artificial intelligence. As for the future directions of TensorFlow development, there are several areas that the TensorFlow team and the wider AI community are actively exploring. Here are some examples:

Unsupervised Learning: TensorFlow is expected to play a significant role in the development of unsupervised learning techniques. These techniques aim to extract patterns and relationships from large, unlabeled datasets, allowing for more efficient and effective learning. Autoencoders, Variational Autoencoders (VAE), Generative Adversarial Networks (GANs), and other unsupervised learning models are already widely used in many applications, and we can expect to see further developments in this area.

Reinforcement Learning: TensorFlow already provides a robust set of tools for implementing reinforcement learning algorithms, but there is still much to be explored in this area. Researchers and developers are working to improve the efficiency and scalability of these algorithms, as well as to develop new techniques for handling complex tasks and environments.

Transfer Learning: Transfer learning is another area where TensorFlow is expected to continue to play a significant role. Transfer learning allows for the reuse of pre-trained models on new, related tasks, reducing the need for large amounts of labeled data and allowing for faster and more efficient training.

Explainable AI: As AI becomes more prevalent in our daily lives, there is a growing need for models that are transparent and interpretable. TensorFlow already provides tools for visualizing and understanding the inner workings of models, and we can expect to see further developments in this area.

Edge Computing: With the increasing prevalence of IoT devices, there is a growing need for models that can be run on the edge, without relying on cloud computing resources. TensorFlow Lite and TensorFlow.js are already widely used for this purpose, and we can expect to see further developments in this area.

These are just a few examples of the many directions that TensorFlow development is expected to take in the coming years. As the field of AI continues to evolve, TensorFlow is likely to remain at the forefront of innovation and progress.